WRITERS
IN THE
KITCHEN

Children's Book Authors Share Memories
of Their Favorite Recipes

Compiled by
TRICIA GARDELLA

Boyds Mills Press

To crafters of words and pictures for children . . .
Past, Present, and to Come
−T. G.

Published by Caroline House
Boyds Mills Press, Inc.
A Highlights Company
815 Church Street
Honesdale, Pennsylvania 18431
Printed in the United States of America

Publisher Cataloging-in-Publication Data
Writers in the kitchen : children's book writers share memories
of their favorite recipes / compiled by Tricia Gardella.—1st.ed.
[256] p. : cm.
Includes index
Summary: Children's book authors and illustrators contribute
recipes and share memories associated with them.
ISBN 1-56397-713-3
1. Cookery, American—Juvenile literature. 2. Literary
cookbooks—United States—Juvenile literature. 3. Authors,
American—Juvenile literature. [1. Cookery, American. 2.
Literary cookbooks—United States. 3. Authors, American.]
I. Gardella, Tricia. II. Title.
641.5972'220—dc21   1998   AC   CIP
Library of Congress Catalog Card Number: 98-70741

First edition, 1998
Book designed by Charlotte Staub
The text of this book is set in Monotype Walbaum

10 9 8 7 6 5 4 3 2 1

CONTENTS

From the minute this idea came to me, I knew this book was going to be fun. I just had no idea how *much* fun—or how enthusiastic the response would be. Not that everyone jumped right in. I was surprised by the numbers who thought they couldn't come up with a recipe and remembrance. But they are creators. All it took was a little memory-bating. Many contributors have thanked me for not letting them off the hook too easily. After the first grumblings, my gentle shove down memory lane seems to have been appreciated, and we've been able to include at least one contribution from every author and illustrator who participated.

Of course, not everyone responded. Some because not all of my requests reached their destination. Others apologized for tight schedules that kept them from contributing. A few of the apologies were just too entertaining to let go, so with permission I have incorporated them into the book.

With each recipe that arrived in my mailbox, I'd wonder anew, "Can it get any better than this?" Not only did it get better, but I was both amazed and pleased by the diversity and creativity. I've been an avid cook for more than four decades, and week after week something new came to me. No wonder literature for children today is so rich.

A special thanks to Lois Lowry, Eve Bunting, and Anna Grossnickle Hines, who believed in my idea enough to share their recipes and remembrances even before there was a contract. I would never have been able to pitch it successfully without them. To Kent Brown for snagging the pitch. And to my husband, Jack, for his patience in this, one of my many enthusiasms he's had to endure in our years together. My meat-and-potatoes ranch man bravely endured—and mostly enjoyed—the taste tests. I know I did. My swelling girth attests to it.

A portion of the proceeds from the sale of this book will go toward the Highlights Foundation Scholarship Fund to help aspiring authors and illustrators toward their goal of sharing their work with children.

Tricia Gardella

Breads

Paul Brewer

In 1953 my family moved from a tiny trailer in a remote Utah canyon to a duplex in the hamlet of Holbrook, Arizona, where my mother had a big enough oven to bake bread. I remember that kitchen well. One red-letter day, with a sound like a bomb, our pressure cooker blew up, erupting hot pinto beans all over the ceiling. My brother and I were agog! This easy, nonexplosive bread recipe came from the Ladies' Home Journal, and we have enjoyed it ever since our Holbrook days. I've baked it from coast to coast, even in a wood-burning oven, and it always makes any kitchen seem like home. With soup and perhaps a bit of cheese we have a complete dinner. It's a batter bread, so it cuts sloppily, especially while warm, and goes dry quickly (that's usually not a problem, since it often vanishes the day it's baked). Any leftovers make wonderful cinnamon toast.

BOOKS BY SUSAN LOWELL INCLUDE:

The Bootmaker and the Elves
Little Red Cowboy Hat
The Three Little Javelinas
I Am Lavina Cummings

Arizona French Bread

2 teaspoons dry yeast
  (or one ¼ ounce packet)
1 to 2 cups lukewarm water
4 cups flour (scooped into
  measuring cup and leveled)

2 tablespoons sugar
2 teaspoons salt
2 tablespoons butter (not
  margarine)

Dissolve yeast in 1 cup lukewarm water. Measure dry ingredients into large bowl and mix with wooden spoon. Add dissolved yeast and beat hard to blend, then add just enough of the second cup of warm water (usually no more than half, depending on the dryness of the flour) to make a soft, rather sticky dough. Cover with towel, and let rise until doubled, about two hours. Punch down, but do not knead—just slap well in the bowl with your hands. This is messy but fun. Scrape into a well-buttered 2-quart glass or pottery casserole dish, or two 1-quart casseroles dishes. Round is best. Let rise until doubled, about an hour. Bake at 400° F for 30 minutes, then remove from oven briefly to brush the top and sides with butter. (Butter is important. With a little on the crust, you don't need any spread on the table; margarine makes dough stick to the bowl. Vegetable spray is better than margarine, but tasteless.) Bake about 10 minutes more, or until loaf sounds hollow when tapped and is deeply browned on bottom.

My grandmother, Margaret Parks, was born in 1901 and grew up on a farm in Missouri. She contributed this recipe to a collection in 1965, with the comment, "I use this in place of both a starch and bread. Simplifies a meal when help is scarce." This has always cracked me up. It speaks of farm life, where the hands needed all the calories they could stomach, including both starch and bread, at that midday meal. And it speaks of that long forgotten time when middle-class people expected "help" in the kitchen. And she didn't mean a microwave, either.

Anyway, this was the dish I begged for from my grandmother's repertoire, which also included chocolate tapioca, lemon cake, and chocolate cookies. She would never make it for Christmas, because it was too "plain." But I got it for every at-home birthday dinner and plenty of ordinary dinners in between. When I grew up and began making it myself, I discovered that the best part is the cleanup, when I get to scrape the sides of the souffle dish for the crunchy part that stuck. I'm sure my fastidious nana never did such a thing. Or did she?

BOOKS BY MARTHA FREEMAN INCLUDE:

The Year My Parents Ruined My Life
Stink Bomb Mom
The Polyester Grandpa

Nana's Spoon Bread

⅔ cup yellow corn meal   1½ teaspoon salt
2 cups milk   ¼ cup butter
1 tablespoon sugar   4 eggs, separated

Preheat oven to 375° F. Grease a 9-inch souffle dish. Stir together corn meal, milk, sugar, and salt in heavy saucepan. Stirring constantly, simmer till thickened—about 10 minutes. Remove from heat and stir in butter till blended. Cool. Beat egg yolks till light and stir in. Beat whites until stiff but not dry; fold in. Bake 35 minutes.

This graham bread was my great-great-grandmother's recipe and is very easy and good.

BOOKS BY SUSE MACDONALD INCLUDE:

Alphabatics

Sea Shapes

Nanta's Lion

Peck, Slither and Slide

Puzzlers

Graham Bread

Preheat oven to 350° F. Butter and flour one bread pan. In mixing bowl, mix thoroughly:

1½ cups whole wheat flour   1½ cups white flour
1 teaspoon baking soda   ½ teaspoon salt

In a 2-cup measuring cup mix:

½ cup molasses   1½ cups buttermilk or sour milk

Add liquid to dry ingredients. Mix and put into pan. Bake for about 65 minutes.

*O*ne of my most favorite treats growing up in a suburb of Pittsburgh was my mother's famous nut and poppy seed rolls. She would often bake, filling the house with all sorts of wonderful smells early in the morning. Of course, there were seven of us kids, so she had to be sure to make enough. We loved having the sliced rolls for breakfast, and it was not hard to make a full breakfast of them.

Years later I insisted that my mother should coach me in the fine art of creating this treat. At first it was a little confusing, but after a few tries they came out great. I wanted to carry on this Ruthenian tradition. During the great immigration of the early 1900s, all of my grandparents traveled to the U.S. from small villages in eastern Slovakia. Like many immigrants, they brought with them many wonderful tastes and traditions. There were all sorts of breads and pastries and many dishes using wild mushrooms, cabbage, beets, ham, and kielbasa. These rolls are especially popular during the holidays of Christmas and Easter. Now, when I'm not visiting family back in Pittsburgh, I get much pleasure in distributing these baked goodies to friends and neighbors.

BOOKS ILLUSTRATED BY JAMES WARHOLA INCLUDE:

Bigfoot Cinderrrella
Bubba, The Cowboy Prince
The Christmas Blizzard
Hurricane City

Ruthenian Nut or Poppy Seed Rolls

FILLINGS: WALNUT: POPPY SEED:

4 cups ground walnuts   2½ cups poppy seed paste
1½ cups milk   ½ cup milk
1 cup brown sugar   1 cup brown sugar

Mix together as to be not too thick and not too liquidy. Add milk as needed.

DOUGH: 2¼-ounce package dry   6 cups flour
            yeast   1 stick butter
        ½ cup warm water   ½ cup sugar
        5 eggs beaten   ¾ teaspoon salt
        ½ cup milk

Dissolve yeast in ½ cup of warm water. Mix together 4 eggs and add milk. Add flour, dissolved yeast, butter, salt, and sugar. Knead. Let rise for 1 hour. Divide dough into six equal parts. Roll out each piece into flat circle. Spread with walnut OR poppy seed paste. Start on one side and roll up. Seal ends and place on greased pan. Brush tops with a beaten egg. Bake at 325° F for 45 minutes, until golden brown. Let cool. Slice to serve.

A BLESSING
By Ivy's daughter, Kim Ruckman Thalman

One November evening in the 1950s
Grandma flipped through the pages
of Ladie's Home Journal *and spotted*
a recipe from the Pillsbury Bake-Off—
Dilly Casserole Bread.

Grandma clucked and read on:
cottage cheese, dill seed, minced onion . . .
That year for Thanksgiving she mixed
and baked her bread in a stainless steel bowl.
Uncle Bill raved.

Each Thanksgiving when Uncle Bill
drove into Hastings and his kids
piled out of the beat-up Cadillac
Grandma would be waiting
with Dilly Casserole Bread.

She popped the bread out of the oven
and it sprang from the bowl,
the top glistening with butter and salt.
She set it on the counter to cool
before slicing the first piece

that fell away like warm cake.
Now when my brothers make it home
for Thanksgiving, Mom bakes
Dilly Casserole Bread and brings it
to the table wrapped in a cloth napkin.

We laugh and talk, remembering how
we used to eat every meal at this table.
I think about how good it feels
to be here, gathered in this circle,
breaking bread together.

BOOKS BY IVY RUCKMAN INCLUDE:

The Hunger Scream
Night of the Twisters
No Way Out

Dilly Casserole Bread

From the kitchen of Grandma Myers

1 package active dry yeast
¼ cup warm water
1 cup cottage cheese lactated to
  lukewarm
2 tablespoon sugar
1 tablespoon minced onion

1 tablespoon butter
2 teaspoons dill seed
1 teaspoon salt
¼ teaspoon baking soda
1 egg
2¼ to 2½ cups flour

Soften yeast in water. In mixing bowl combine cottage cheese, sugar, onion, butter, dill seed, salt, baking soda, egg, and softened yeast. Add flour to form a stiff dough, beating well after each addition. (For first addition of flour, use mixer on low speed.) Cover. Let rise in warm place (85-90° F) until light and doubled in size, 50 to 60 minutes.

Stir down dough. Turn into well greased 8-inch round (1½ to 2-quart) casserole dish. Let rise in warm place until light, 30 to 40 minutes. Bake at 350° F for 40 to 50 minutes or until golden brown. Brush with butter; sprinkle lightly with salt.

When my children were small we lived in a 150-year-old farmhouse in upstate New York. The lack of insulation made the house difficult to keep warm, so on cold winter days cooking projects were always popular. ABC pretzels were a favorite recipe. My daughter and son loved to squish the flour and water between their fingers as they kneaded the dough. Then they tore off chunks, rolled them into strips, and bent them into letters. With a little help, even my three year old could form the M, A, T, T of his name. After the pretzels were cooked, Matt proudly ate them one at a time, saving the M for last. (These pretzels resemble the soft, Philadelphia-style pretzels that you can eat with mustard.)

BOOKS BY CAROLINE ARNOLD INCLUDE:

African Animals
Hawk Highway in the Sky
Stone Age Farmers Beside the Sea
Bobcats
Bat

ABC Pretzels

1½ cups water	1 tsp salt
1¼-ounce package dry yeast	1 egg, beaten slightly, with
4 cups flour	1 tablespoon of water
1 tablespoon sugar	coarse (kosher) salt

Dissolve yeast in the water. Mix together flour, sugar, and salt. With a large spoon work flour mixture into yeast mixture in a large bowl. When about 3 cups of flour have been worked in, begin to knead mixture on counter while working in the remaining flour.

Divide the dough into 18 to 24 parts. Shape dough into letters and place on greased cookie sheets. Paint with egg-water mixture and sprinkle with salt. Bake 15 minutes at 425° F.

Whenever we visited my grandma, she made these biscuits as a special treat. The smell of them baking was delicious in itself, but even better was eating the biscuits when they were almost too hot to hold. They were the first bread I learned to bake, and the fun of rolling dough in my hands and neatly knotting it (or not so neatly at first) introduced me to the comfort of baking. Grandma kept on making these biscuits as her contribution to family dinners even after she was too old to cook anything else. Now in her 90s, she doesn't bake them anymore. But whenever we have a family gathering, one of the grandchildren is sure to bring Grandma's Biscuits.

BOOKS BY MARISSA MOSS INCLUDE:

Regina's Big Mistake
Knick Knack Paddywack
In America
Amelia's Notebook

Grandma's Biscuits

¼ pound margarine (one stick)	1 egg
5 tablespoons sugar	1 package yeast
1 teaspoon salt	4 cups flour
1 cup boiling water	poppy seeds

1. Put margarine, sugar, and salt in bowl. Pour boiling water over mixture. Mix till margarine melts. Add egg, stirring well.

2. In another bowl mix together yeast and flour. Add flour mixture to egg mixture, one cup at a time, till dough can be handled (you may not need all four cups).

3. Place dough in greased bowl, punch down, turn over and cover with towel. Let rise in warm place for one to two hours.

4. Punch down dough, divide, and roll into long strands between the palms of your hands (like challah braids). Shape each strand into a knot. Let rise in warm place until size is doubled.

5. Brush with milk and sprinkle poppy seeds on top. Bake approximately 10 minutes at 400° F. Makes about 2 dozen biscuits.

Grandma's Old World recipes ... homemade jams ... Sunday feasts with cousins and neighbors ... spaghetti sauce cooking at a sputtering simmer. What memories! Too bad they aren't mine. When I think about my childhood, food does not figure into the picture. Going to the lake, flooding the side yard for a skating rink, buying my first fifty-cent Nancy Drew, rescuing worms in a rainstorm—the details of those adventures are clear and ready for retelling. But when it comes to food, I'm stumped. I have four wonderful children. When one developed an interest in baking she knew instinctively she was on her own. So, if you can't turn to Mom for great recipes, where do you go? The Internet. My daughter, Ellen, makes these delicious, gorgeous, knock 'em-dead cinnamon rolls from scratch! (I can't tell you how this astounds me that I have a child who knows what to do with yeast.) She got the recipe from one of my cyber-pals, Sheila Arvin, whom I met through an Internet literary society devoted to that wonderful children's author, Maud Hart Lovelace. Enjoy.

BOOKS BY MARSHA QUALEY INCLUDE:

Everybody's Daughter
Revolutions of the Heart
Come in from the Cold
Hometown
Thin Ice

Ellen and Sheila's Fab Cinnamon Rolls

DOUGH: 1 tablespoon dry yeast   ½ cup melted butter
           1 cup warm milk   1 teaspoon salt
           ½ cup white sugar   2 eggs
                         4 cups flour

Dissolve yeast in warm milk. Add the rest of the ingredients and mix well. Knead into a ball. Let rise until doubled in size. When ready, roll out to about ¼ inch thick. Spread with filling as described below:

FILLING: ¼ cup butter, softened   1 cup brown sugar
                     3 tablespoons cinnamon

Spread butter on dough evenly. Sprinkle sugar and cinnamon over dough evenly. Roll up dough. Slice into 1-inch slices. Place on a greased pan, bake about 12 minutes at 400° F.

ICING: ½ cup butter, softened   1 ounce cream cheese
           1½ cups powdered sugar   2 tablespoons whipping cream
                     1 teaspoon vanilla extract

Beat until fluffy. Spread icing on hot rolls.

I *didn't cook much when I was young. You see, I lived in the southwest corner of Ethiopia where we had no grocery stores, no refrigerator until I was older, and only a wood-burning stove to cook on. School boys, who had to come a long distance to get any kind of education, worked for my family to help make money to pay their school expenses. They went to the markato to buy ingredients, killed chickens in the backyard, and did most of our cooking, supervised by my mother.*

When I was in seventh grade, though, my older sister was sent to high school in Egypt. That Christmas, my mother flew off to spend the holiday with her. We often had guests—the Scottish nurse who supervised the clinic by our house, the American teacher who supervised the school, ferenji (foreign) visitors to the area, or Ethiopian friends. But who would cook for our Christmas tea?

Well, I would! I followed a recipe for the first time to bake a cowboy coffee cake. My father and the school boys must have helped with the wood-burning stove. I don't remember much about putting the cake together, but I do remember that everyone who came to tea said it was delicious.

BOOKS BY JANE KURTZ INCLUDE:

Trouble

Only a Pigeon

Miro in the Kingdom of the Sun

Pulling the Lion's Tail

Fire on the Mountain

Cowboy Coffee Cake

2 cups flour

4 tablespoons sugar

3 teaspoons baking powder

½ teaspoons salt

1 egg, slightly beaten

6 tablespoons shortening

⅔ cup milk

Mix together dry ingredients. Cut in shortening. Stir in liquid ingredients. Press into greased 9-inch round or square pan.

Mix following ingredients:

¼ cup flour

¼ cup butter

¼ cup brown sugar

1 teaspoon cinnamon

⅓ cup chopped walnuts

(optional)

Spread on top of batter. Bake at 400° F for 25 minutes.

One of the jobs I've had that I wasn't fired from was in a sweet-smelling bakery during my college years. I sold delicious breads and pastries. Unlike other aspects of my life, this one hasn't led to any books so far. But perhaps it's one reason I was attracted to writing a book about the Mexican celebration of Days of the Dead—because I got to include a recipe for the gaily decorated, cakelike bread known as Pan de los Muertos or "Bread of the Dead." This anise-flavored dessert is sold in Mexican markets during this celebration, the same time of year as the American Halloween, along with sugar skulls and amusing skeleton toys. My husband, Paul Brewer, and I were married on Halloween—another reason I was inspired to write Maria Molina and the Days of the Dead, and we collect art from this holiday, especially skeleton brides and grooms. The Days of the Dead are a hopeful time, a flavorful celebration of family history. To honor relatives who have died, the bread can be decorated with angel faces or with little knobs of dough to represent the bones of the dead or the tears of the living. Unique!

BOOKS BY KATHLEEN KRULL INCLUDE:

*Lives of the Artists: Masterpieces, Messes
(And What the Neighbors Thought)*

*Lives of the Musicians: Good Times, Bad Times
(And What the Neighbors Thought)*

*Lives of the Writers: Comedies, Tragedies
(And What the Neighbors Thought)*

*Lives of the Athletes: Thrills, Spills
(And What the Neighbors Thought)*

*Wilma Unlimited: How Wilma Rudolph
Became the World's Fastest Woman*

Pan De Los Muertos or Day of the Dead Bread

From her book Maria Molina and the Days of the Dead.
Drawing by her husband, Paul Brewer.

Grease a large cookie sheet.
Mix the following ingredients in a large bowl until smooth:

2 cups all-purpose flour	⅔ cup milk
2 teaspoons baking powder	¼ cup vegetable oil
2 tablespoons sugar	10 drops anise extract
¼ teaspoons salt	(a licorice-like flavoring)
1 egg	

With clean hands, either mold the dough into one large round shape with a raised knob in the middle, or break the dough into smaller amounts and make many round shapes. You can also mold the dough into the shapes of animals, faces, or angels. Place the dough on the cookie sheet.

In a smaller bowl, mix these ingredients for the topping:

¼ cup brown sugar	1 teaspoon ground cinnamon
1 tablespoon all-purpose flour	1 tablespoon melted butter

Sprinkle topping on dough. Bake at 400° F for 20 to 25 minutes. Serve warm with milk.

I *came from a family of recyclers. Clothes were passed down. Gift wrapping, bows, and boxes were saved and reused. Then, if we could not recycle something ourselves, we gave it to Goodwill or the Salvation Army.*

This banana bread recipe is the "Best Ever," because it takes ugly, squishy yellow-black bananas and recycles them into a delicious loaf dessert. And to keep the "recycle" theme going in my own family, we live in the country. With goats, pigs, horses, chickens, ducks, dogs and cats around, no scrap of food is ever wasted here. Even banana peels are gobbled up!

BOOKS BY LINDA JOY SINGLETON INCLUDE:

Love to Spare
Opposites Attract
Teacher Trouble

Best-Ever Banana Bread

½ cup margarine	bananas
1 cup sugar	2 cups sifted flour
2 eggs	1 teaspoon baking soda
3 large overripe	1 teaspoon cinnamon

Cream margarine and sugar in a bowl. Beat in 2 eggs. Add mashed bananas to mix. Sift together flour, soda, and cinnamon. Add to mixture in bowl. Add chopped nuts if desired. Pour mixture into greased and floured bread pan. Bake 350° F for 50-60 minutes.

TOPPING: 1 teaspoon melted butter   ½ teaspoon cinnamon
1 tablespoon sugar

Topping: Pour melted butter over warm, baked banana bread. Sprinkle mix of cinnamon and sugar over buttered bread.

I *still smile when I remember the sights, sounds, and smells of our family Christmases: the sight of little white lights twinkling, the joyful sound of carolers, the pine smell of our Christmas tree. We made strings of popcorn for decorations and sent our school pictures in Christmas cards we made from paper dipped in melted crayons. Right now, I can almost smell the spicy pumpkin breads baking in our oven.*

My mother baked a dozen or more pumpkin breads every December morning (four at a time, in one-pound coffee cans). No, we didn't eat them all. After the breads cooled, my mom removed them from the cans and wrapped them in aluminum foil. Then she wrapped each with a sheet of clear, red- or green-colored cellophane and tied it on with a ribbon.

My dad owned a real estate business. He loved taking pumpkin bread to work each day to give to clients and friends. They made bright, tasty Christmas gifts. Now my brother owns the business and my sister-in-law and I carry on the tradition. Nothing takes the place of warm, spicy pumpkin bread. Mmmm . . . can you smell it, too?

BOOKS BY GLENDA PALMER INCLUDE:

Blue Galoshes
P is for Pink Polliwogs

Pumpkin Bread

Sift together and set aside:

3½ cups flour	2 teaspoons soda
1½ teaspoons cinnamon	½ teaspoon salt
1 teaspoon nutmeg	

Cream together:

3 cups sugar	⅔ cup water
1 cup pumpkin	⅔ cup oil
4 eggs	1 tablespoon vanilla

Mix in dry ingredients and add:

¾ cup raisins	1 cup chopped nuts

Pour into four 1-pound coffee cans, greased and floured. Fill half full. Bake at 350° F for 60 minutes. Remove from cans when cool. Wrap in aluminum foil and tie on colored cellophane for gifts. Breads may be stored in cans with plastic lids or frozen.

Breakfast

One of the best memories I have is of my mom's French toast on Saturday mornings, with her dash of vanilla that made it so special. I have to confess, it was a dud when I served it to a French family visiting me. They commented all the way through breakfast about how "unusual" our American tastes were—cooking bread and eating bacon with "sweet" food. Oh well. Nobody else has ever complained!

BOOKS BY BARBARA SEULING INCLUDE:

From Beginning to End
Freaky Facts
Monster Mix

Mom's French Toast

8 slices of bread	1 teaspoon cinnamon
1 or 2 eggs	1 teaspoon sugar
½ cup milk	1 teaspoon vanilla

Mom used plain-old white bread, but you can be creative. Oatmeal works nicely, as do some of the multi-grains. The bread shouldn't be too dense or it won't soak up the egg/milk mixture too well.

1. Beat well. (Mom, always economical, made one egg stretch, but I use two for more than four slices of bread.) Add milk, cinnamon, sugar, and vanilla extract to eggs. Beat well. Rebeat each time you dip in a new bread slice, to keep the cinnamon blended evenly.

2. Melt approximately 1 teaspoon of butter or margarine in large skillet for each batch. If you can fit four slices in the pan at once, you may need slightly more butter, but a film covering the pan should be enough.

3. Dip bread slices in mixture. Let them soak for about 15 seconds on each side, long enough to absorb some of the liquid, but not long enough to get soggy.

4. Drain bread slices and place in hot buttered skillet over medium heat.

5. Cook until bread is golden brown and turn over. Cook until other side is browned.

6. Serve immediately with butter and maple syrup and bacon, if you dare.

Waffles were an old-fashioned family affair that occupied our Saturday mornings long before we owned a television—and ages before we ever dreamed of spending a morning in front of one! Still in pajamas, my sister, Peggy, and I would climb onto stools in our tiny kitchen to help Mom assemble bowls, utensils, and ingredients, while Dad lined up the electric waffle iron—a huge, wobbly contraption that looked like something borrowed from the local car repair shop.

Peggy and I took turns helping. After Mom separated the eggs, I beat the whites, then Peggy beat the yolks; then I poured the milk while Peggy helped Mom measure the dry ingredients; then I sifted, then Peggy sifted, until we'd created a tidy floury mound on a piece of waxed paper. We took turns again to mix the batter with the rotary beater while Mom added the oil. Finally, she supervised our technique as we folded the fluffy egg whites into the batter.

Meanwhile, Dad waited by the hot iron muttering incantations to prevent the waffles from sticking. They always did, but no one cared. Even in pieces, they were the best waffles in the world.

BOOKS BY SUSAN HART LINDQUIST INCLUDE:

Walking the Rim
Wader

Mother's Saturday Waffles

2 eggs, separated	3 teaspoons baking powder
1½ cups milk	½ teaspoon salt
1½ cups flour	6 tablespoons oil
½ cups corn meal	

Separate the eggs. In a small bowl, beat egg whites until fluffy. Set aside. In a large bowl beat yolks, then add milk and blend. Measure and sift dry ingredients. Add slowly to the egg and milk mixture and beat. Stir in oil. Carefully fold in the egg whites. Mix well. Pour by large spoonfuls onto hot waffle iron.

How I hated breakfast! Hated eggs. Hated bacon. Hated oatmeal. Hated milk with my cereal. Hated bagels and lox. Forget about bread and butter.

My mother despaired. So that I would eat something, unusual servings might appear, including pies and cakes. Best of all—my father's favorite: fried potatoes and onions. Now this was breakfast! I loved it and couldn't wait for it to be served. Hardy. Aromatic. Tasty. Comfort food. Consumed on indolent Sunday mornings.

Today I often return to the meals of my youth and the memories inherent within them; when food wasn't always nutritious but still good for you; when we all sat around a Sunday breakfast table reading the funnies; thus, a morning repast of last night's meal (although more halibut then dessert), of fried potatoes and onions, albeit with a 90s flair. As a mom, I am grateful I am not emulated by my children in these peculiar habits (my daughter loves oatmeal—arrghhhh!). But this is the meal of my early home. Of my parents. It is the meal I retain as I go forward in life, still not terribly fond of breakfast, still without milk in my cereal.

BOOKS BY SARA JANE BOYERS INCLUDE:

Life Doesn't Frighten Me
O Beautiful for Spacious Skies

Breakfast Potatoes and Onions

A simple breakfast for all those kids (like me)
who don't like breakfast foods

As a child:	margarine	3 or 4 potatoes
	2 or 3 large onions	

As an adult: *(adding to above ingredients)*

	garlic	mushrooms
	peppers (large green, red, or yellow)	

To taste:	pepper	dried rosemary or fine herbs

As a child I would eat simple fried potatoes and onions prepared as follows (and washed with a glass of my mother's freshly squeezed orange juice):

Peel potatoes and slice into half-moon shapes (unless small). Slice onions.

Melt margarine in a skillet. When it bubbles, add sliced potatoes. Cook until they are translucent. Add onions. Cook both potatoes and onions until onions are richly brown and potatoes are well cooked and brown. Remove, blot on paper towels and eat (with or without ketchup).

When I cook this now I alter the recipe as follows (and my kids often eat it washed down with homemade watermelon/banana/orange juice/yogurt/berry smoothies):

After margarine is hot, sauté a mashed clove of garlic (unless you have a major meeting in the morning) before adding potatoes. I usually add to above recipe whatever I find in the refrigerator: peppers, broccoli, mushrooms, carrots . . . even apples! And while cooking, I season with rosemary, fine herbs, and perhaps some pepper. I don't cook with salt, but it may be added. I will often serve with a hot sauce, perhaps some parsley, or just plain ketchup. Still a great breakfast to me!

My mom has always loved to cook, so we often were surprised at dinner with her latest great recipe discovery or experiment. When she made egg baskets, I was really impressed. This seemed like such a gourmet dish to me with its own sauce and pastry—and I wasn't an egg eater. In fact, it was a chore to get them into me. Maybe that's why she made this dish. Hmmmmm, tricked into eating something I didn't like. Oh, mothers can be so sneaky!

BOOKS BY JUDITH ROSS ENDERLE INCLUDE:

Six Sleepy Sheep
Two Badd Babies
The Good-for-Something Dragon
Upstairs

Egg Baskets

1½ cups flour
½ teaspoon salt
½ cup vegetable shortening

⅓ cup shredded cheddar cheese
5 to 6 tablespoons water
paprika (optional)

Sift dry ingredients into a mixing bowl. Cut in vegetable shortening and cheddar cheese. Work until the particles are the size of small peas.

Sprinkle 5 to 6 tablespoons water over the mixture a little at a time while tossing and stirring lightly with a fork. Work until the dough is just moist enough to hold together. Form into a flat ball. Roll out to 1/8 inch thick. Cut out six circles (5 inches across). Fit each inside a greased muffin pan or individual tart pans, pressing the pastry against the bottom and sides. Pastry should extend slightly above the rim. Cut out six more circles (4 inches across). Reroll dough if necessary. Cut an X in the center of each small circle.

Break 6 eggs into the pastry-lined pans. Sprinkle each lightly with salt and pepper. Cover each with a small pastry circle and seal the edges by pinching to form a rim. Sprinkle with paprika, if desired.

Bake at 450° F for 20 minutes, until golden brown. Serve hot with sauce.

SAUCE:

⅓ cup butter or margarine

⅓ cup flour

2½ cups milk

½ cup shredded cheddar cheese

2 tablespoons chopped parsley

2 teaspoons dill seed, crushed

½ teaspoon salt

Melt butter or margarine in a pan. Blend in flour, then gradually add milk. Cook over low heat, stirring constantly until thickened. Remove from heat and stir in cheese, parsley, dill seed, and salt.

D*espite comments from my husband, David, that all Swedish food is soft, white, and overcooked, my childhood memories consist of good dishes with interesting names that I never learned to spell. I only recently learned that rora means gravy.*

Both of my mother's parents were Swedish, and the two-family house was conducive to the regulation coffee-and-cake together every afternoon, and to the gathering of aunts, uncles, and cousins every holiday. I realize now how much work went into those meals, especially since my mother was employed as an at-home typist. But my memory prefers to think it all happened easily, with lots of surrounding fun and laughter.

Agg Rora was a special breakfast. I preferred it (and still do) with crisp bacon broken into little pieces scattered on top. It's a good dish for the morning after a pajama party, or a late night supper, and the host may want to get everyone involved by letting each take turns stirring it.

By the way, it is Swedish. And soft. And white. But you really can't overcook it. As for the spelling—well . . . !

BOOKS BY LYNEA BOWDISH INCLUDE:

Living with My Stepfather is Like Living with a Moose
This is Me, Laughing
A Friend for Caitlin
Downey and Buttercup's Adventure
The Carousel Ride

Agg Rora

| 3 eggs | 3 tablespoons butter or margarine |
| 1½ cups milk | 3 tablespoons flour |

Mix together butter and flour in a warm, large frying pan with high sides. Stir over heat until blended. Add eggs and milk to flour mixture. Cook slowly until thick, stirring constantly (this will take a while). Add more milk if it gets too thick. Add salt and pepper to taste. When you are finished, the mixture should be thick and creamy rather than lumpy.

Dayton Hyde's mom's recipe for perfect pancakes:

1. majestic wood stove
2. maple wood
3. pancake batter
4. blueberries, syrup, and butter
5. tender loving care

BOOKS BY DAYTON HYDE INCLUDE:

The Major, the Poacher, and the Wonderful One-Trout River
Don Coyote
Island of the Loons

Soup, Salads, Sandwiches

Brian Selznick

I am not known for my cooking. I'm known for my Christmas cookies and poppy seed bread and I like to make homemade soup, but beyond that, I'd rather eat out. When I was a teen-ager, I was friends with a girl named Iggie who had lost her mother when she was small. Raised by her father, perhaps like Alice in my books, she and her dad did all the cooking. When I found myself in her home for lunch one day, this was what she made. I thought it delicious. Actually, what I remember most about that lunch for two was that we told each other some very personal stuff. I was probably so interested in what I learned from Iggie that anything would have tasted good. I think I've made it once or twice since then, but nobody else thought much of it.

BOOKS BY PHYLLIS REYNOLDS NAYLOR INCLUDE:

Shiloh
Alice-in-Between
Unexpected Pleasures
The Keep
I Can't Take You Anywhere

Pots of Gold

biscuit baking mix	water
can of tomato soup	small cubes of cheddar cheese

Mix soup and water. Heat on stove. Meanwhile, mix up some dough according to package directions. Roll into small balls and insert a cube of cheese in each, molding the dough around it. When soup is simmering, drop the balls of cheese-filled dough into the soup and simmer until the dough seems cooked. Serve in soup bowls.

When I was a kid, I hated anything green. My parents couldn't get me to eat peas, beans, broccoli, or zucchini. I detested salads. The only vegetable I would touch was carrots, so they fed me them at every meal. I ate so many carrots, I'm surprised I didn't grow pointed ears and a cotton tail!

You can imagine how thrilled I was when I had my own family and discovered this recipe for Carrot Soup. It was easy to prepare, and my four children loved it as much as I did. They loved the taste. They loved the smoothness and the soft orange color. And they loved that it was just as good served hot in the winter as it was served cold in the summer.

But I loved something more. Having finally learned to like green vegetables, I discovered that I could use frozen spinach, broccoli, and any leftover vegetables in my refrigerator instead of the carrots and still have a delicious soup. And so my children suggested I call this recipe Carrot, or Whatever, Soup.

BOOKS BY ANN WHITFORD PAUL INCLUDE:

Eights Hands Round: A Patchwork Alphabet
The Seasons Sewn: A Year in Patchwork
Shadows are About
Silly Sadie, Silly Samuel
Everything to Spend the Night

Carrot, or Whatever, Soup

2 cups peeled, diced potatoes
1¼ cups sliced carrots (or any
　　other favorite vegetable)
1 leek, sliced (mostly white part)

3 cups chicken broth
1 cup cream (heavy, half-and-
　　half, or plain milk)
salt and pepper to taste

Combine the potatoes, carrots, leek, and chicken broth in a saucepan. Bring to a boil. Reduce heat and simmer for about 30 minutes. Puree soup in a blender. Add cream, then salt and pepper to taste. Serves 4.

M*y mother died when I was twelve years old, leaving my two younger sisters and me in my father's care. He was a farmer who somehow managed to rear us three with no outside help. He often made Optional Soup, so called because he used whatever vegetables were available. It always had potatoes and cabbage. Sometimes he added bits of meat left over from the chicken he had roasted for Sunday dinner.*

One of my fondest memories is arriving home from school on cold, snowy winter days to find a pot of Optional Soup simmering on the stove. It nourished both the body and the soul.

BOOKS BY ANN TOMPERT INCLUDE:

Saint Patrick
The Jade Horse, the Cricket, and the Peach Stone
Grandfather Tang's Story

Optional Soup

Place in a large kettle:
        3 tablespoons of cooking oil
Sauté:
    4 cups of hot water or stock   ½ cup of pared, diced turnips
    1 cup of canned tomatoes   ½ teaspoon of salt
    ½ cup of pared, diced potatoes   ⅛ teaspoon of pepper

Cover and cook about 20 minutes or until vegetables are tender. Then add ½ cup chopped cabbage. Cook about 5 minutes more. Season to taste. Serve with thick slices of French bread.

Patricia Lee Gauch

This is not authentic, in a way. I love the name of this soup, of course, and it warmly reminds me of authentic. My father, a home-cooking kind of connoisseur of good food, loved ground beef dishes. They were like steak to him. Or prime rib. Or a rack of lamb. There was nothing better. My mother used to make a Riding Hood-like dish my father called Slumgullion. It came in a soup bowl, and into it we could add ketchup or mustard or onions or any other delicacy. Conversation always grew spirited over Slumgullion, because we were happy that just the right meal had been set before us. We would have more than one bowl and would debate and argue and tease heartily with this meal in front of us. You might want to bone up on current affairs and sharpen your debating skills. Conversation and Little Red Riding Soup (or Slumgullion!) simply go together.

BOOKS BY PATRICIA LEE GAUCH INCLUDE:

Christina Katerina and the Box
Christina Katerina and the Time She Quit the Family
Dance, Tanya
Thunder at Gettysburg
This Time, Tempe Wick?

Red Riding Hood Soup

1 pound ground beef	1 package dry onion soup
2 cans tomato sauce	4 beef bouillon cubes
2 cans stewed tomatoes	1 to 4 tablespoons sugar (to taste)
2 packages brown gravy mix	2 packages frozen mixed vegetables
4 cups water (or more)	

Brown meat and drain. Add tomato sauce, stewed tomatoes, brown gravy mix, water, dry onion soup, beef bouillon cubes, sugar, mixed vegetables, and pearl barley. Simmer for 1 hour. Serves 8.

I *was a lucky child. My mother was a writer, a playwright, and author of juvenile books. I considered this second in pleasures only to having a mother who owned a bakery. Mom tested new ideas and practiced plots on us, her four children, and we delighted in recognizing friends and neighbors, slightly altered, as characters in her books.*

Whenever I heard the Underwood typewriter clacking on the sun porch and smelled the Inspiration Soup simmering in the kitchen, I knew a book deadline was approaching. Mom always filled the kettle with soup enough to nourish her family until she'd typed, "The End," wrapped her manuscript in brown paper, secured it with string, and sent it on the road to New York City. Then we all celebrated the end of the book and of the soup by making a batch of Toll House cookies.

The Inspiration in the recipe's title comes from using whatever leftovers the refrigerator offers. Every potful was an original, for Mom, a sensitive writer, couldn't reject anything.

BOOKS BY SHIRLEY CLIMO INCLUDE:

City! New York
City! San Francisco
Stolen Thunder: A Norse Myth

Inspiration Soup

2 pounds of Polish kielbasa or
    Italian sausage, cubed
1 medium onion, chopped
1 cup carrots, sliced
1 cup celery, sliced
2 potatoes, cubed
1 large can (28 ounces) tomatoes,
    broken up with a fork

6 to 8 cups of stock (beef,
    chicken, or vegetable)
1 or 2 cloves of garlic, minced
1 teaspoon brown sugar
1 teaspoon red wine vinegar
    (or some red wine if it's handy)

In a large kettle, brown sausage and drain off fat. Add remaining ingredients and simmer for about 45 minutes. Then put in any or all of the following, whatever inspires you:

1 cup noodles, or any other cooked pasta
green beans (kidney beans or black beans are good, too)
corn (fresh, canned, or frozen)
zucchini
2 or 3 cups shredded spinach or cabbage, or a combination
of both

Cook for an additional 15-20 minutes. Cool. Season with salt and pepper to taste, and add about a tablespoon of chili powder if you like it (I do). Serve with French bread and pass a bowl of Parmesan cheese.

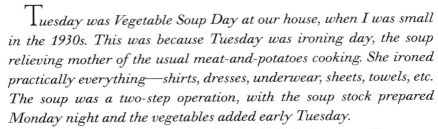

Tuesday was Vegetable Soup Day at our house, when I was small in the 1930s. This was because Tuesday was ironing day, the soup relieving mother of the usual meat-and-potatoes cooking. She ironed practically everything—shirts, dresses, underwear, sheets, towels, etc. The soup was a two-step operation, with the soup stock prepared Monday night and the vegetables added early Tuesday.

Soup was served about noon, after which the hobos came. They were among the millions of homeless during the Great Depression who rode the rails. Our house was on a corner, and we could look out the window and see the hobos walking up the sidewalk. There were at least four, sometimes more, and they sipped soup and ate bread in our backyard. Mother called them "victims" of the Great Depression.

A popular pastime in the thirties was to go to the railroad station and watch the trains arrive. We could see hobos in the boxcars, or sometimes lying on top, and wondered if any of them were "our hobos." The hobo culture ended in about 1941, with the beginning of World War II.

BOOKS BY COLLEEN STANLEY BARE INCLUDE:

Busy, Busy Squirrels
Critter: The Class Cat
Love a Llama

Beef-Vegetable Soup

BEEF STOCK:

3 pounds lean beef (chuck, shin, brisket, etc.) cut into 1-inch pieces
1 large soup bone, cracked
5 quarts cold water
salt
2 sliced onions
5 carrots, cut in large pieces
3 stalks celery with leaves
seasonings: thyme, parsley, bay leaves

Put beef, bone, water, and salt into large pot; simmer two hours. Add remaining ingredients and simmer another 1½ hours. Remove from heat, remove bone, and strain. Cool, store in refrigerator. When cold, skim fat off top.

Reheat stock, then add:

1 small head cabbage, chopped

1 bunch carrots, scraped and sliced

3 onions, diced

several ribs of celery, cut in small pieces

2 cans tomatoes

1 chopped turnip

Any other vegetables will also do: fresh peas, beans, potatoes, spinach, leeks, etc. Can also add ½ cup pearl barley or rice.

Bring to boil, simmer about an hour or until vegetables are tender. (Modern technology: this freezes well).

*F*or me, the recipe that conjures up the fondest childhood memories would have to be my dad's natural broth quahog (hard-shell clam) chowder. It brings back the sights, sounds, and smells of summer— seagulls on the wing, the briny smell of the sea, the laughter of children, kites in the air, sailboats zipping across the bay, a whiff of suntan lotion—all the joys of a summer day.

When I was a child we rented a small cottage July Fourth week every year on a small island in Buzzard's Bay, on Cape Cod. It was there, and only there, that my dad made his chowder. It seemed that the car would no sooner be unpacked than my dad would be in his swim trunks, and the annual ritual would begin. He'd head for the beach, rake in hand, with all four of us kids in tow. It was almost like a treasure hunt for us, squishing our toes in the muck, feeling for the prize of a quahog shell. We competed to see who could find the most, pausing only to partake in the inevitable seaweed fight. When the bucket was full, my dad would return to the cottage to peel and dice and chop, while my mom basked in the sun, enjoying the break from her usual cooking chores, and the rest of us frolicked on the beach. When we returned in late afternoon, sandy, sunburned, and hungry, the big old kettle would be bubbling, and the steam would be rich with the salty scent of the sea. After all that, though, none of us would touch a clam—not even my mom. Dad would ladle out big bowls brimming with broth and potatoes, and these we would gobble, but heaven forbid that a clam should touch our lips. Dad never minded, though. "More for me," he always said with a smile.

About fifteen years ago my dad and mom retired to the Cape, just a couple of miles from the island. A few years after that my husband and I bought one of the little cottages on the island, and we've summered there with our children ever since. My parents are still well, fortunately, and Dad continues to make his chowder for our annual July Fourth picnic. He still puts in lots of extra potatoes for the kids and my mom, but I've finally discovered what he was smiling about when he said, "More for me." Needless to say, Dad doesn't get all the clams anymore.

BOOKS BY JACKIE FRENCH KOLLER INCLUDE:

No Such Thing
A Dragon in the Family
Mole and Shrew

Dad's Crowd-Size Cape Cod Quahog Chowder

a bucket of quahogs   8 cups diced potatoes
(about 10 quarts)   1 cup dry vermouth or water
8 ounces salt pork   2 cups chopped onion

Scrub quahog shells with a wire brush until clean. Discard any clams that are partially open. Place clean clams in a lobster pot. Add one cup of vermouth or water. Cover and steam slowly over medium heat until all clams are open. Cool. Remove clams. Set clam liquid aside. Cut clams into chunks. Place in colander and squeeze under running water to clean. (Skip this step if you like the clam bellies.) Chop rinsed clams.

Slice salt pork into thick chunks and sauté slowly in a small bit of olive oil in lobster pot for about 30 minutes. Add onion. Cook until tender. Remove salt pork and put clams back in. Add potatoes. Cover with clam liquid, adding more water if necessary. Cook until potatoes are tender. Add pepper to taste and salt, if needed (not usually necessary). Enjoy!

I *love soups, especially soups that are the whole dinner—yum! This recipe is from my father-in-law, George Wayland. One year, thinking about what to give his grown children for the holidays that would be meaningful, he decided to put all of their favorite family recipes on computer and then to print them out and put them in a notebook for each. Our copy of this book of family recipes has been much loved and much used.*

BOOKS BY APRIL HALPRIN WAYLAND INCLUDE:

It's Not My Turn to Look for Grandma Booth
Night Horse
To Rabbittown

Grandpa's Potato-Bean Soup

½ cup sliced celery
2 medium shredded carrots
1 clove minced garlic
2 teaspoons melted margarine
4 cups chicken broth
3 medium peeled and cut up
   potatoes

2 teaspoons dried dill weed
1 can (15 ounces) drained Great
   Northern beans (they are white)
½ cup nonfat yogurt
1 tablespoon all-purpose flour
salt and pepper to taste

In a large saucepan cook and stir celery, carrots, and garlic in hot margarine over medium heat for 4 minutes or until tender. Carefully stir in broth, potatoes, and dill. Heat to boiling, reduce heat. Simmer, covered, 20 to 25 minutes or until potatoes are tender. With the back of a spoon, lightly mash about half of the potatoes in the broth. Add the drained beans to the potato mixture.

In a small bowl, stir together yogurt, flour, pepper and salt (salt is optional); stir into potato mixture. Cook and stir until thickened and bubbly. Cook and stir 1 minute more. Makes 4 to 6 main dish servings.

When I was growing up, my sister, brother, and I would always ask "What's for dessert?" as soon as we sat down to eat supper. That's because we each had a sweet tooth and would have preferred to skip the rest of the meal. Vegetables were not popular with us.

My mother used to make this soup, and we ate it with no complaints. Since we couldn't see the vegetables, we didn't really know what it was we were eating. All we knew was that it tasted good. This is a hearty soup, and served with some good bread, it can make a whole meal. But it's even better if there is a yummy dessert to eat after it.

BOOKS BY JOHANNA HURWITZ INCLUDE:

Aldo Peanut Butter
Make Room for Eisha
Yellow Blue Jay

My Mom's Pea Soup

8 cups water	pepper
one small onion	2 cups green split peas
one carrot	fresh parsley
small bunch of celery	6 frankfurters
salt	

1. Fill large kettle with 8 cups of water and place over low heat.
2. Cut up and add onion, carrot, celery, using both tops and bottoms. Add salt and pepper to taste.
3. When water boils, add 2 cups of green split peas, which have been rinsed, but not soaked.
4. Cook on low heat for about 90 to 120 minutes, until all the vegetables are soft and split peas are dissolved.
5. Grind vegetables with liquid through a food mill or puree in blender or food processor. Add some fresh parsley through the grinder.
6. Cut up frankfurters and add to the soup.

*I*n another cookbook I called black beans the aristocrats of beans, and I was right, for they are among the most full flavored of beans as well as more expensive than most. They are my favorite beans.

Ned and I like black bean soup so much we served it at our wedding reception. It's difficult to believe such ordinary ingredients could turn out so ambrosially. Enough olive oil to float an armada is one of its secrets, but it is good with less, too.

BOOKS BY CRESCENT DRAGONWAGON INCLUDE:

Brass Button
The Dairy Hollow House Cookbook
Annie Flies the Birthday Bike

Cuban Black Bean Soup

cooking spray
2 cups dried black beans, washed and picked over
2½ quarts any well-flavored vegetable stock or water
2 bay leaves
1 fresh jalapeño pepper, chopped with seeds (if you want the soup
   just a little hot, remove the seeds and white pith from the pepper)
¼ to ¾ cup (if conscience allows) olive oil
3 large onions, chopped
2 green bell peppers, stemmed, seeded, and chopped
4 to 6 cloves garlic, peeled and put through a garlic press or finely
   chopped
salt to taste
1½ to 2 cups cooked white rice, for serving
1 onion, chopped, for serving

1. Spray a large heavy soup pot with cooking spray and in it soak the beans in stock or water to cover overnight.
2. The next day add enough of the remaining stock or water to cover the beans by 1 inch. Add the bay leaves and jalapeño, cover the pot, and bring to a boil. Turn down the heat to very low and let simmer, partially covered, until the beans are tender, about 1 ½ to 2 hours.

3. Meanwhile, in an 8- or 9-inch skillet, heat the oil over medium heat. Add the onions and green peppers and sauté until softened, about 3 minutes. Stir in the garlic and cook a few seconds more.

4. When the beans are tender, add the onion mixture to them and season with salt. Let simmer another 20 minutes. Serve at once, or, even better, the next day. Pass the rice and chopped onion at the table. Serves 6 to 8 as an entree.

VARIATIONS:

- To make this soup with canned beans, pour 5 cans (15 ounces each) of black beans with their liquid into a heavy soup pot and add an equal amount of vegetable stock. Add the bay leaves, broken up a bit, and heat through. Then proceed as directed, adding diced jalapeño to the pepper-onion sauté.

- Déjà Food: A little black bean soup, like any bean soup, is wonderful stirred into any vegetable soup. If you have a lot leftover, you could make Ned's Mother's Casserole, a dish he loved as a child: ground beef browned with chopped onions and layered with mashed potatoes and black bean soup, then baked. He thinks maybe there was grated cheese on top. Nowadays, though, we are more likely to cook the soup down and use it to fill enchiladas. Every couple of years we do the calorically irresponsible but divine Mock Turtle Soup with Black Beans: Measure leftover black bean soup into a food processor. Add 1 ½ teaspoon dry sherry and 2 to 4 tablespoons heavy cream for every cup of soup. Puree, then heat through. When ready to serve, stir in half a hard-cooked egg white, diced, for each cup of soup, and garnish the soup with the crumbled yolk. This is so good it's almost overkill.

- Black bean soup is delicious and attractive garnished with a few slices of ripe avocado, too.

BOOKS BY ROBERT SAN SOUCI INCLUDE:

The Samurai's Daughter
The Talking Eggs
Sukey and the Mermaid
The Faithful Friend
Nicholas Pipe

Holiday Swirl Soup

yellow squash cut into large
   chunks, approximately 3 cups
1 tablespoon fresh ginger root,
   finely chopped

1 to 2 cups vegetable or chicken stock
1 cup cream, milk, or soy milk
3 to 4 red beets
1 bunch spinach

Steam squash until tender. Remove peel. Blend with ginger and stock. Set aside. Juice raw spinach and raw beets separately in electric juicer. You are creating edible paints to work with.

Heat squash soup over medium heat. Add more stock or water if necessary, or milk if a creamier soup is preferred. Serve into wide bowls. Spoon in a dollop of beet juice, and a dollop of spinach on the opposite side. Serve the soup with a chopstick to be used to swirl the colors around. Those eating the soup love to get creative before eating it; some make one simple swirl, others keep going until it is a complex mess, but all have fun making a work of art, not to keep, but to eat! It's a colorful soup, easy to make, very nutritious, and interactive!

Sheri Cooper Sinykin

E*ver since I began learning to speak Spanish in the sixth grade, I dreamed of visiting Spain. Little did I know that my dream would come true only three years later. The summer after my freshman year in high school, I was fortunate to travel and study there with a group of students. I especially loved the Andalusia region of southern Spain, with its whitewashed buildings, red-tiled roofs, and rich history. Most magical of all was the palace and fortress of the Moorish kings of Granada, the Alhambra, which I used as a setting in my Magic Attic Club series book,* Viva Heather! *My favorite food discovery that summer of first independence was gazpacho, a chilled tomato-based soup that has a delicious crunch and a garlicky bite. In the more than thirty years since my first trip to Spain, I've searched high and low for a gazpacho recipe that would bring me back to my fifteenth summer. Ironically, I finally found it during a recent birthday dinner in my own hometown.*

BOOKS BY SHERI COOPER SINYKIN INCLUDE:

The Secret of the Attic
Trapped Beyond the Attic
The Shorty Society
Sirens
Slate Blues

Gazpacho

From the Restaurante La Paella, Madison, Wisconsin

4 ripe tomatoes	2 ounces olive oil
½ small onion	2 ounces red wine vinegar
1 cucumber	2 slices of bread
1 clove garlic	salt and pepper to taste
1 medium red pepper	

For garnish: chopped tomato and cucumber

Combine all ingredients together in a blender. Puree until smooth. Refrigerate until well chilled. To serve, garnish with chopped cucumber and tomato. Serves 4.

In some circles, my caesar salad is more famous than my body.

BOOKS BY JAMIE LEE CURTIS INCLUDE:

When I was Little: A Four-Year-Old's Memoir of Her Youth
Tell Me Again About the Night I Was Born

JLC "Famous" Caesar Salad

garlic salt
2 heads romaine lettuce (cut away top and bottom quarter of lettuce
    and slice into 1-inch pieces)
2 handsful of freshly grated Parmesan cheese

Combine and set aside:

¼ cup olive oil	½ teaspoon dry mustard
20 shakes worcestershire sauce	salt
2 lemons	pepper
2 cloves garlic, pressed	

CROUTONS:

4 pieces sliced sourdough bread, cubed

Coat skillet generously with olive oil then heat till smoking. Add
bread and toss continuously till golden brown (reduce heat if burning).
Put bread on paper towels and sprinkle with garlic salt.

THE SALAD:

Combine all of the above just before serving, tossing the lettuce well.

I remember making a special salad dressing for Christmas. The whole family sat in the kitchen chopping and dicing the ingredients. My mother was fussy about the size things were to be chopped—quarter inch cubes, no larger. I liked doing the celery best of all. Five long cuts down the length of the stem one-quarter inch wide, then nice clean crosscuts one-quarter inch wide. My father was the most precise. Cutting the green pepper was his specialty. When everything was ready—green pepper, celery, and pimentos—they were placed into sterile Ball jars, making beautiful red and green Christmas colors. My mother mixed a big batch of oil, vinegar, sugar, and Heinz chili sauce, which made a smooth, luscious sweet-and-sour brew. It was poured over the ingredients in the Ball jars—red, green, and white vegetables bathed in the rich, red sauce. The jars were sealed and put in the refrigerator. We would spoon it over crisp hearts of lettuce, or eat it by the spoonfuls right out of the jar.

BOOKS BY TED LEWIN INCLUDE:

I Was a Teenage Professional Wrestler
Amazon Boy
Market!

BOOKS BY TRINA SCHART HYMAN INCLUDE:

How Six Found Christmas
A Little Alphabet

Clean-Out-Your-System Spring Salad

*You must live in the country or in a garden-type community
to be able to make this salad. The original recipe came
from the fairies of The Bavarian Countryside—
or so my mother told me.*

In equal portions:

dandelion leaves, picked before the dandelions put out flowers
violet leaves
violet flowers and buds
sunflower seed sprouts or radish sprouts
fiddlehead Ferns (cooked and drained) or fresh raw asparagus,
cut into 1-inch lengths*
tiny new potatoes (steamed and cut in quarters)

Additional ingredients:

small pitted black olives (out of a can, drained)
chive flowers and fresh chives, chopped into ½-inch lengths

Dressing:

½ cup green olive oil
¼ cup white rice vinegar (or 2 tablespoons lemon juice)
1 teaspoon maple syrup (or honey)
1 or 2 cloves of garlic, chopped fine or mashed
some salt and lots of fresh ground pepper

Almost all of the salad ingredients can be found in your own back-yard, if you live outside the city, have a patch of garden, and feed the birds. The perfect time to gather the ingredients in New England is during the last weeks of April or the first weeks of May. This is exact-

---

*Fiddleheads—the fern before it unfolds—must be from the ostrich fern. Scrub off all the brown paperlike covering. Wash well and steam or simmer for 7 to 10 minutes. Rinse under cold water and drain.

ly the time your body is screaming to put on new wings and fly—and this salad will help you do it.

The dandelion leaves and violet leaves at flower are high in vitamin C and potassium and are also more interesting and delicious than any lettuce or mesclun you've ever tasted.

The sunflower sprouts can be found, for free, under your bird feeder. The fiddleheads are found in any swampy, ferny patch in New England—or use substitute fresh asparagus, which has something of the same taste (but not the magic).

M*y mother believed it would bring good luck if you ate black-eyed peas on New Year's Day. Hey, don't knock it. I've eaten them every New Year's Day of my life, and I've had great luck. I even call my kids the day before and remind them to eat their black-eyed peas. They've had good luck, too.*

In the past few years, I've had a New Year's Day supper for friends, and instead of regular black-eyed peas, I serve this salad. It works just as well and tastes even better. Good Luck!

BOOKS BY BETSY BYARS INCLUDE:

The Summer of the Swans
The Pinballs
Wanted . . . Mud Blossom
The Burning Questions of Bingo Brown
The Dark Stairs, A Herculeah Jones mystery

Black-Eyed Pea Salad

2 cans black-eyed peas (water packed, no pork)
$\frac{1}{2}$ cup rice vinegar
2 teaspoons sugar
$\frac{1}{4}$ teaspoon dry mustard
$\frac{1}{2}$ cup sliced green onions (some tops)
2 cups chopped tomatoes

Drain peas and rinse. Combine vinegar, sugar, and mustard. Stir till dissolved. Pour over peas and onions. Refrigerate for at least a couple of hours. Before serving, add tomatoes, and stir lightly. Serves 6 to 8.

My mother loved making salads. Most of the time she'd make what she called her plain salads—lovely affairs with lettuce and tomato and radish and avocado. But once in a while, on a Sunday, she'd make one of her fancy salads. Here is one such Sunday salad that I especially enjoyed (and it's so simple to make!).

BOOKS BY JEANNE MODESITT INCLUDE:

Vegetable Soup
Mana, If You Had Wish
Sometimes I Feel Like a Mouse: A Book About Feelings
Lunch with Milly
The Mice Family Celebrate Chanukah

Sunday Salad

1 jar (6 ounces) marinated artichoke hearts
1 cup fresh (or frozen) peas

Steam peas until tender, about 5 minutes. Mix with artichoke hearts and serve. Serves 2 to 3.

When I was a kid, Thanksgiving wouldn't have been Thanksgiving without Grandma's Heavenly Hash. My cousins thought it was her pumpkin pies, but what did they know? They were from the city. We had Grandma year round in her tiny home next door. But on Thanksgiving her entire family gathered. Talk about stuffing. The dining room, the kitchen, and the living room, all with their tables and chairs. We kids spent the morning watching out the window for the arrival of the city cousins. And every year they spent their entire visit letting us know we were country hicks. Then they'd go home, and we'd begin counting the days until they came again. Now that we're all grown up, I'm still a country hick. And I have a feeling the cousins always wished they could be, too.

BOOKS BY TRICIA GARDELLA INCLUDE:

Just Like My Dad

Casey's New Hat

Heavenly Hash

½ pint whipping cream	1 can fruit cocktail
3 tablespoons sugar	1 cup seedless grapes
¼ cup maraschino cherry halves	½ cup chopped walnuts (optional)
1 small can mandarin oranges	shredded coconut (optional)
1 can pineapple chunks	

In separate bowl, whip cream until stiff. Fold in sugar. Combine next five ingredients (plus walnuts, for those who like a bit of a crunch.) Fold whipped cream into fruit mixture. Serve in one large bowl or in individual sherbet glasses. Sprinkle top with coconut, if desired. About 8 servings.

My grandmother was a wonderful cook—challah, stuffed peppers, homemade French fries, chicken soup. I remember watching her braid bread and set a Romanian corn meal pudding to steam. Sadly, none of her recipes were handed down to my mother or me.

My diet nowadays is largely vegetarian (with some fish and seafood thrown in). I sometimes make pretty fancy fare—poached salmon, chocolate souffles, artichoke pâté. But mostly I eat a lot of pasta and rice dishes. I don't like meat now, and I didn't much like it when I was a kid, either. Years ago, to escape from our frequently carnivorous fare, I came up with these simple childhood meals.

BOOKS BY MARILYN SINGER INCLUDE:

Big Wheel
Family Reunion
The Painted Fan

Asparagus Sandwiches

8 spears of asparagus   a little olive oil
two slices of bread (round sourdough or crusty Italian is best)
slices of hard cheese, such as Gouda or fontina

Trim the asparagus stems. Steam the spears until just soft. They should still be green. Brush a small amount of olive oil on the bread. Lay four stalks of asparagus on each slice. Cover with cheese. Melt under a broiler. Serves 1. This sandwich is great with tomato soup and a mixed green salad.

Cream Cheese-and-Olive Sandwiches

cream cheese   two slices of bread (pumpernickel or rye is good)
$\frac{1}{8}$ cup black or green olives, chopped

Spread cream cheese thinly over the bread. You don't need a thick layer. Sprinkle each slice with the chopped olives. If you want a saltier taste, use pitted Kalamata olives. Serves 1. Also good with soup and a salad.

At eight years of age, my list of preferred foods was short, simple, and nonnegotiable:

Heinz spaghetti, from a little can; peanut butter; spinach (don't ask); white American cheese, each piece individually rinsed in warm water.

Now, when I say white cheese, I mean that I refused orange. Yuck! The mere sight of it disgusted me. Unluckily, my father had the opposite opinion. The upshot was a formal taste test; kind of like the gunfight at the OK corral, only different. I was securely blindfolded and made to sit at the kitchen table, a piece of white cheese in one hand, a piece of orange in the other. Which was which? While confident of my ability to recognize my beloved white, I was petrified of biting into that foul orange.

But the moment was nigh. "1, 2, 3 - go!" shouted my father.

I prayed quickly, moved a random hand to my mouth, and bit. "White!" I yelled, in relief. "It's white!"

I heard a snicker. I dropped the cheese and tore off the blindfold. A horrible sight met my eyes: the white piece of cheese, whole and beautiful. That was the last time I ate orange cheese.

BOOKS BY NANCY WERLIN INCLUDE:

Are You Alone on Purpose?

"War Game" in Twelve Shots: Outstanding Short Stories about Guns, edited by Harry Mazer

Cambridge Gothic

Pure, Uncorrupted Grilled Cheese Sandwiches

Irresistible for the picky eater!

two slices of normal white bread   real butter, and lots of it
2 to 3 slices of cheese (never orange)

1. Between two slices of bread, place enough cheese to melt into a gooey mess.
2. Melt butter in a heavy flat pan on the stove.
3. Place sandwich in pan.
4. Mash sandwich down heavily with spatula. Use all your weight.
5. Listen to sizzling.
6. In a little while, peek to see if the first side has turned golden brown. Keep peeking until it has.
7. Flip sandwich in a professional manner using spatula. Beginners can use a fork.
8. Cook other side.
9. Again wielding spatula expertly, transfer sandwich to plate.
10. Briskly cut sandwich once, diagonally, corner to corner. If you get this wrong, your sandwich is inedible.

Jean Van Leeuwen

When I was a child, the long lazy days of summer vacation were the time when I went to the library, got as many books as I was allowed to take out, and draped myself on the couch or the porch to read. On those hot days, my favorite lunch was a lettuce and tomato sandwich. The bread was fresh from the downtown bakery, and the tomatoes were fresh picked from my father's garden. I haven't had this sandwich for years, but in my memory it is the perfect lunch for a hot summer day.

BOOKS BY JEAN VAN LEEUWEN INCLUDE:

Amanda Pig, Schoolgirl (of the Oliver and Amanda Pig series)
Emma Bean
Bound for Oregon
Dear Mom, You're Ruining My Life
Blue Sky, Butterfly

Summer Reading Sandwich

2 slices fresh-baked white bread   3 to 4 slices home-grown tomatoes
as much lettuce as you like   mayonnaise to taste

Slather mayonnaise on a slice of bread. Arrange tomato and lettuce on the bread. Put second slice of bread on top. Cut and eat with a glass of milk and a good book.

Brenda Z. Guiberson

M*y father used to make grape sandwiches when I was very young.*
My favorite place to eat them was outside, where I shared them with
the dog or any other creature that happened to come by.

BOOKS BY BRENDA Z.GUIBERSON INCLUDE:

Cactus Hotel
Lighthouses
Lobster Boat

Grape Sandwiches

Grapes: red, purple, green, or black
Cheese, your favorite kinds

Wash grapes. Drain. Pull off stems and cut in half. Remove seeds if
any are present. Carefully cut cheese into thin squares or rectangles.
Plop cheese onto a grape half, add the top, and the tiny grape sandwich
is ready to eat.

Ashley Bryan

*When it comes to cooking and recipes from any age ... I'm sunk!
I have no mind for cooking and couldn't begin to spell out a recipe
for anything beyond ... and barely ... a toasted cheese sandwich!*

BOOKS BY ASHLEY BRYAN INCLUDE:

*Ashley Bryan's ABC of African American Poetry
The Ox of the Wonderful Horns: And Other African Folktales
The Story of Lightning and Thunder*

Variations on the Grilled Cheese Sandwich
In Honor of Ashley Bryan

GRILLED CHEESE AND MUSHROOMS:

Sauté ½ cup sliced fresh mushrooms in butter and garlic. Arrange 1 slice sour dough bread with slices of cheese of choice (sharp cheddar is yummy). Add sauteed mushrooms. Cover with second slice of bread. May be grilled in buttered frying pan or under the broiler.

GRILLED CHEESE AND ORTEGA CHILIES:

Arrange 1 slice sour dough bread with slices of Monterey Jack cheese. Spread with canned, chopped Ortega chilies. Cover with second slice of bread.

May be grilled in buttered frying pan or under the broiler.

GRILLED PEPPER CHEESE AND TOMATOES:

Arrange 1 slice sour dough bread with slices of Monterey Jack pepper cheese.

Spread with chopped tomatoes. Cover with second slice of bread. May be grilled in buttered frying pan or under the broiler.

GRILLED CHEESE WITH BACON:

Fry two slices bacon until crisp. Arrange 1 slice sour dough bread with slices of cheese of choice. Cover with second slice of bread. May be grilled in buttered frying pan or under the broiler.

GRILLED CHEESE WITH APPLES:

Arrange 1 slice sour dough bread with slices of cheese of choice. Add apple, slice (Granny Smith work well). Cover with second slice of bread. May be grilled in buttered frying pan or under the broiler.

GRILLED OPEN-FACED CHEESE SANDWICHES:

Toast a slice of sour dough bread. Spread with pizza sauce or salsa. Cover with grated cheese of choice. Place under the broiler until cheese bubbles

I *can't think of anyone less qualified to contribute to a cookbook than myself. Instant oatmeal is about my speed. Plus, I learned it all from my parents, who couldn't be bothered either. If it weren't for peanut butter and jelly, I might not be here today.*

BOOKS BY MARK TEAGUE INCLUDE:

The Field Beyond the Outfield
Frog Medicine
Pigsty

Variations on the Peanut Butter Sandwich
In Honor of Mark Teague

What memories of childhood do not at some point include peanut butter?

Using bread of choice, and remembering to spread the peanut butter all the way to the crusts. . .

peanut butter and sliced bananas
peanut butter and sliced oranges
peanut butter and chopped celery
peanut butter and sliced tomatoes
peanut butter and grated carrots
peanut butter and sliced cucumbers
peanut butter and minced green pepper
peanut butter and mayonnaise, bacon, and lettuce
peanut butter and sweet red onion
peanut butter and dill pickle
peanut butter and marshmallow creme

Vegetables and Side Dishes

Lisa Desimini

F*ew things take me back to my growing-up days on Shallowford Road in Chattanooga like the smell of a pot of greens on the stove. I live in the North now, and since Yankees, God bless their deprived culinary souls, know scant little more about cooking greens than they do about barbecue (most Yankees think barbecue is a verb), it is a rare occurrence except in my kitchen. This recipe is equally fine for turnip greens, though not for more delicate greens like kale or spinach.*

BOOKS ILLUSTRATED BY BARRY MOSER INCLUDE:

Appalachia: The Voices of Singing Birds

Alice's Adventures in Wonderland

*A Ring of Tricksters: Animal Tales from North America,
the West Indies, and Africa*

Greens

2 or 3 large bunches of fresh collard (or turnip) greens. (In the lean winter months one may have to resort to frozen greens, which is okay).

a large pot of water

1 or 2 ham hocks (smoked ham hocks are particularly good. A piece of Steak-o-Lean also works well. In a pinch, a few teaspoons of bacon fat will suffice.)

3 or 4 tabasco peppers (any very hot small pepper will do, fresh or put up, or if you're brave, chop or crack the peppers before putting them in the pot.)

1. Wash the greens thoroughly. (I know people in Mississippi who put their greens in a mesh bag and wash them in the delicate cycle of the washing machine—without soap, of course.

2. Chop greens and place in a large pot.

3. Add water to fill the pot. Leave 2 to 3 inches at the top so it doesn't boil over.

4. Bring to a hard boil.

5. Add ham hocks and 4 or 5 tabasco peppers.

6. Reduce to a simmer and go away. You cannot overcook collards. The worst thing that can happen is to let the water boil away, which burns the greens and makes them inedible. By the same token, the water should not be replenished for any reason other than the above, because the fluid that remains on the bottom (which is called *pot-likker*) is an excellent condiment for corn bread, the ordained natural accompaniment.

Serve piping hot with a few splashes of hot pepper vinegar. Greens are splendid with pork, fried or baked chicken, or barbecue, but barbecue is an entirely different matter.

Thinking back on my childhood, there are few things I remember more clearly than being sent out by my grandmother, Marion Bowman, to gather a mess of dandelions. Grampa Jesse would loan me his pocketknife. Even though I was only a small child, he'd hone it sharp as a razor and trust me to know how to use it right.

Early spring is the time to gather dandelions, before they form their first blossoms, when they are young and tender and greener than the grass itself.

The trick is to dig the knife in and cut around the base so that some of the pale root comes out with the whole plant, the leaves still attached. A mess is about a quart pan full of dandelions.

The moist smell and feel of the grass, the gritty sound a knife makes as it cuts through roots and sandy soil, and the songs of the warblers in the basswood tree at the edge of the woods remain part of my own personal recipe for making those greens taste sweet.

A lawn full of dandelions is a homeowner's curse today, but to Grama and Grampa and me it was another way the best things in life were just given us by our Creator, free.

BOOKS BY JOSEPH BRUCHAC INCLUDE:

Bowman's Store, an autobiography
Lasting Echoes
Tell Me A Tale, A Book about Story and Storytelling
Many Nations: An Alphabet of Native America
Dog People

Dandelion Greens

One quart or so of fresh dandelion greens. Rinse well. Place in a saucepan. Cover with cold water. Boil at medium heat until tender. Drain off water and add butter and salt to taste.

My dad, Lester Kroll, whom I call Fath, tells me that his German-born parents hired neighborhood children to pick dandelions for them. They used fresh leaves in soups, salads, or as a side dish. The flowers were the main ingredient in my Grandpa Kroll's potent dandelion wine.

My father says that he learned many culinary tricks from the French. He was stationed there as a special agent in the Counter Intelligence Corps during World War II. He enjoyed his exotic dishes and the fact that he was, during the 1950s, one of the few fathers who cooked. He explained that most of the great chefs were men, and to this day he encourages us to "do as the French do: Don't simply eat. Dine."

BOOKS BY VIRGINIA KROLL INCLUDE:

Hands

Butterfly Boy

Masai . . . and I

Fath's Dandy Dandelions

dandelion leaves	2 tablespoons brown flour
1 small onion	olive oil, butter, or vegetable oil
1 clove garlic (or garlic salt)	water

For each person you plan to serve, pick a handful of dandelion leaves. They shrink quite a bit as they cook. New leaves without flowers tend to taste better, as do those in shaded areas. Separate any grasses and stems from leaves and rinse leaves well. Cut or rip into bite-sized pieces, as you would salad greens. Steam for about 5 minutes (or until tender). Peel and dice onion. Finely chop garlic (or use one teaspoon garlic salt).

Coat the bottom of a frying pan with oil. Combine onion, garlic, and flour, stirring constantly until a gravy forms. Add water for desired consistency. Add cooked leaves to gravy and stir until they are coated.

This is a recipe from my mother, who can't cook. Our family always laughed about this, even as we suffered through another tough brisket or soggy eggplant parmigiana. So, who would have guessed that one of the most popular dishes every Thanksgiving, among all of our extended cousins and aunts and grandparents, would be a dish by my mother? Well, not exactly by my mother . . . You may have seen it on the side of mushroom soup cans in the grocery store but never thought about making it. It's Mushroom String Bean Casserole, and man, is it good!

This is my mother's slight variation on the actual recipe, as she remembers it. She still makes it; we still like it. Hope you do, too.

BOOKS ILLUSTRATED BY BRIAN SELZNICK INCLUDE:

The Houdini Box
Dollface Has a Party

Thanksgiving Surprise

4 cans (10 ¾) ounces) each condensed cream of mushroom soup
4 16-ounce cans of cut string beans
1 cup milk (more or less if you'd like, says my mom)
1 large can fried onion rings (Divide into two equal
    halves. Set one half aside.)
  dash of pepper

Mix everything together (except ½ can onion rings) in oiled casserole dish.

Cover. Bake in a 350° F oven for 20 minutes. Uncover. Pour remaining onion rings on top. Bake uncovered for 10 more minutes.

Serves 6 to 8 . . . and be glad I didn't give you the brisket recipe.

During the time we lived in an old house in Sonoma County (the one that inspired the Westerly House in my book, The Headless Cupid), we always had a large vegetable garden that, for some reason, was dominated by enormous zucchini plants. From year to year we always seemed to forget how prolific they were, and the result was a great superfluity of zucchinis. We ate vast amounts and gave so many to friends, relatives, and colleagues that my husband became known as the zucchini pusher of Sonoma State University.

BOOKS BY ZILPHA KEATLEY SNYDER INCLUDE:

Black and Blue Magic
And All Between

Zucchini Frittata

*The following was a favorite among the many, many recipes
we tried during those years of zucchini surplus.*

2 tablespoon butter or margarine	$\frac{1}{2}$ cup water
$\frac{1}{4}$ cup thinly sliced green onion	$1\frac{1}{4}$ teaspoon seasoned salt
2 cups thinly sliced fresh zucchini	$\frac{1}{8}$ teaspoon Tabasco
8 eggs*	$\frac{1}{2}$ cup finely diced fresh tomato

Melt butter in skillet that is oven safe. Add onion and zucchini and sauté quickly, until barely tender. Beat eggs just to blend whites and yolks; stir in water, salt, and Tabasco. Pour over zucchini in skillet; sprinkle tomato over top. Let cook on medium heat for about 5 minutes, then bake in 350° F oven for 20 to 25 minutes, or until eggs are set and top is dry. Makes 4 generous servings, approximately 232 calories and 13 grams of protein per serving.

*May use egg substitute for eggs.

My mother was raised by Irish in Illinois, but her cooking was jazzed up by tricks she learned during her student year in Paris. We ate vegetables cooked until just barely tender and seasoned with fresh herbs. Corn, the pride of Illinois, was a favorite of ours. It was sometimes prepared in a pressure cooker. Once, the cooker exploded. My warmest memories are of Sunday supper: popcorn. My father took over, when he was around, popping quantities of corn and pouring melted butter and salt over it. Then we all sat around the kitchen, this family so often angry and miserable, and laughed ourselves silly listening to Jack Benny, Our Miss Brooks, and the rest of the comedy line-up on the radio.

BOOKS BY EMILY ARNOLD McCULLY INCLUDE:

Mirette on a Highwire
Starring Mirette and Bellini
Popcorn at the Palace

Succotash

Combine in saucepan, or double boiler, 1 or 2 cups cooked corn and equal amounts of cooked lima beans, butter, salt, paprika, any minced fresh herbs. Heat through.

I *grew up in a French-Italian household where food was king! My mother came to this country from France, not knowing how to speak English or how to cook. She learned to do both in the kitchen of my Italian grandmother. There were animated "discussions" at the table as to which was better: French or Italian cuisine. We loved everything that concerned food: shopping for it, preparing it, eating it, critiquing the meal, comparing it with previous ones, comparing it with that of this aunt or that one, and then planning the next one. A fine meal with friends was one of life's simple joys. "Treat your family as guests, and your guests as family," was my mother's credo. This recipe has been in the family for generations. My brother and I still prepare it for our family and friends.*

BOOKS BY DIANE GOODE INCLUDE:

Diane Goode's Book of Giants & Little People
Mama's Perfect Present
Where's Our Mama?
The Little Book of Nursery Animals

Roasted Red Peppers and Black Olives

4 tablespoons extra virgin olive oil
2 fresh garlic cloves, crushed
6 red bell peppers, roasted, peeled, seeded, and torn into broad lengthwise strips

¼ cup black pitted olives, crushed
2 tablespoons capers, rinsed
2 tablespoons pine nuts
1 tablespoon seasoned bread crumbs

In a large skillet, heat oil over high heat. Add garlic cloves. Remove from heat when they turn golden brown. Add red peppers, olives, capers, and pine nuts. Reduce heat to moderate. Cook, stirring occasionally until the peppers are heated through. Sprinkle bread crumbs over the peppers and remove from heat. Transfer to a serving bowl. Serve warm or at room temperature with big chunks of crusty, fresh Italian bread.

Here is my favorite recipe from my childhood, even though it's quite possible I did not really eat it as a child.

BOOKS BY PETER SIS INCLUDE:

Komodo!
A Small, Tall Tale from the Far, Far North

Sauté onion, garlic, and celery (sliced thin) in hot oil. Add lentils (green lentils, if possible) and stir to coat well. Sauté another minute or two.

Add pieces of ham, bacon, or salami—cut into small cubes, pepper, bay leaf, marjoram, and 3 cups of water. Cover and simmer for 30 minutes. Drain, remove bay leaf. Add vinegar, sugar, salt (1 spoonful each), bit of mustard.

When my daughter became a vegetarian, we did a lot of experimenting in the kitchen. This recipe is a result of that, and also of experimenting with menus for Sheep Out to Eat. In imagining how my characters could make mistakes in a restaurant, I tried out (on paper!) many combinations of foods, searching for rhymes and the maximum ee-ewe! quotient. I featured spinach custard because it sounds awful, but as a crustless quiche, it could taste pretty good. You can use reduced-fat cheese and milk, or substitute other cheeses.

BOOKS BY NANCY SHAW INCLUDE:

Sheep in a Jeep

Sheep on a Ship

Sheep in a Shop

Sheep Out to Eat

Sheep Take a Hike

Spinach Custard

1 small onion, chopped (optional)	1 cup milk
¾ cup shredded mozzarella cheese	1½ teaspoon dried basil, or
10-ounce package frozen spinach,	4 teaspoons fresh
thawed and squeezed to reduce	½ teaspoon oregano
excess moisture	¼ teaspoon thyme
3 eggs	¼ teaspoon garlic salt

Place onion, cheese, and spinach in food processor and blend. Add remaining ingredients and blend again. Pour into a greased 9-inch pie pan and bake at 375° F for about 30 minutes, until it has puffed and slightly browned, and a knife inserted in it comes out clean.

*O*nce a year, on Thanksgiving, my mother would make tomato pudding, a sweet, rich concoction with a marvelous texture. The pudding was so rich my mother insisted that a small spoonful was a serving, but I was willing to risk a stomachache for several heaping spoonfuls. Although the pudding was very sweet, it was always served as a side dish to the main course; the dessert course was reserved for pies. This is a simple recipe with just a few ingredients and delicious results. But remember, a small spoonful is a serving, although I never did suffer a stomachache from my extra helpings.

BOOKS BY DENISE FLEMING INCLUDE:

In the Tall, Tall Grass
Count!
Lunch
In the Small, Small Pond
Barnyard Banter

Tomato Pudding

1 cup brown sugar	2 cups toasted bread cubes
1 cup tomato puree	½ cup melted butter
¼ cup water	

Preheat oven to 325° F. Combine sugar, tomato puree, and water in saucepan. Boil 5 minutes. Place toasted bread cubes in small casserole dish. Pour butter over bread cubes. Pour tomato mixture over butter and bread cubes. Bake in oven for 50 minutes.

Every Thanksgiving, while my mom prepared Thanksgiving dinner, my dad took us kids by subway to Manhattan, where we'd plant ourselves by the curb near Broadway and 34th Street to watch the Macy's Thanksgiving Day Parade. When we came home, cold and tired and hungry, dinner was ready: turkey, of course (except for one year, probably during World War II, when we had a capon instead), some vegetable, such as green beans or peas, and this yummy dish that my mom always referred to as "Lincoln Sweets." I asked her once where the name came from and she couldn't remember. Years later, after she died and I was looking through her belongings, I found an envelope with yellowed recipes in it. One, a raggedy page from a pamphlet, was a recipe for "Lincoln Sweets."

BOOKS BY BARBARA SEULING INCLUDE:

From Beginning to End
Freaky Facts
Monster Mix

Lincoln Sweets

4 medium-sized sweet potatoes	½ cup brown sugar
4 medium-sized apples	butter
½ cup granulated sugar	bread crumbs

1. Preheat over to 400° F. Butter a deep baking dish.
2. Wash sweet potatoes thoroughly and boil until tender.
3. Meanwhile, pare, core, and slice the apples and place them in a saucepan with the granulated sugar and just enough water to keep from burning. Cover and steam over low heat for 15 or 20 minutes.

Peel potatoes and cut lengthwise in thick slices. In baking dish, place a layer of sliced potatoes, dab with bits of butter and sprinkle with brown sugar. Add a layer of apple. Repeat until all the ingredients are used. Sprinkle top with breadcrumbs, add a few dabs of butter, and bake in oven for 15 minutes.

My mother got this from a home economics teacher, and she and I continued to adapt it. While originally you were supposed to simmer for an hour (get real!), then bake for one to two hours in a 300° F oven, I always mix, then microwave on high for as long as it takes to cook the hamburgers (or whatever). My family likes it just fine!

BOOKS BY CHERYL BYRD ZACH INCLUDE:

Benny and the Crazy Contest
Benny and the No-Good Teacher

Quick Baked Beans

2 #2 cans pork and beans
1½ teaspoons vinegar
⅓ cup dark corn syrup
1 to 2 tablespoon chili powder, depending on taste
1 tablespoons dried chopped or minced onion
¼ teaspoon dry mustard
2 slices bacon
1 cup water (only if you really cook it in oven for 2 hours)

Combine ingredients into casserole dish. Lay bacon slices on top. Bake—see above—in oven or microwave. Serves 6 to 8, or my kids and friends.

Never mind matzo as the food of the poor slaves who raced out of Egypt without time to let the bread rise. For us, matzo balls came to represent my mother's power to turn humble food into something light enough to ascend into heaven. Each Passover we sat in eager anticipation for this dish. At last it arrives, the steaming bowl of chicken soup with the large, loosely shaped matzo ball that always threatens to disintegrate in the liquid. Spoon cuts ball in half and encounters nothing but sweet softness throughout. Tastes as good as it feels. No chewy matzo balls in this house!

How did she do it? She gave me the recipe. I made matzo balls. Sometimes almost as good, sometimes quite ordinary, a few times like golf balls. My sons said the right thing, but their eyes said, "These aren't Nana's."

The family gathered at our house for the seder one year. The matzo balls were set before each person. My mother divided and devoured hers first. I stopped breathing. With amazement she proclaimed, "Malka, the matzo balls are wonderful." Everyone echoed her sentiments.

BOOKS BY MALKA DRUCKER INCLUDE:

The Family Treasury of Jewish Holidays
Frida Kahlo: Torment and Triumph in Her Life and Art

Matzo Balls

I've used Manischewitz Matzo Mix, but if you'd like to try
my mother's recipe, here it is:

5 well-beaten eggs
6 tablespoons cold water

1 cup matzo meal
5 tablespoons rendered chicken fat

Mix ingredients together in a large bowl. Cover and put in the refrigerator for 4 hours. Bring 4 quarts of water to a boil. Roll mixture into little balls and drop into the boiling water. Cook covered for 30 minutes. This makes 10 to 12 matzo balls.

When *I was growing up, every year during the winter school break we would drive from Montreal to Brooklyn, New York, to visit my mother's family. Grandma Annie was always waiting for us with a platter of Hanukkah latkes. Her tiny, warm apartment would be suffused with a wonderful frying onion smell. To this day, every time I make potato latkes I become my grandmother, transformed by the aromas and memories. But I always feel as if I'm cheating, using my handy food processor. Grandma scraped those potatoes laboriously by hand, a true labor of love.*

BOOKS BY JOANNE ROCKLIN INCLUDE:

For YOUR Eyes Only!
The Case of the Missing Birthday Party
The Case of the Backyard Treasure

Potato Latkes (Pancakes)

4 potatoes, peeled	1 teaspoon salt
3 to 4 eggs	freshly ground black pepper
1 large onion	pinch of baking soda
¼ cup flour	vegetable oil

Grate the potatoes in a food processor, then grate the onion. Insert the steel blade in the processor and add the rest of the ingredients, except the oil. Pulse just until mixed. In a large skillet (or you can use two skillets and fry two batches at once, for speed) heat ¼ inch of oil. (Oil must be hot.) Spoon large tablespoons of potato batter into the hot oil, flattening with the back of a spoon. Brown, turning only once. Drain on paper towels. (You can keep the latkes warm in a low oven as you fry the remaining batter.) Serve with sour cream and applesauce.

Yield about 2½ to 3 dozen latkes, depending on their size.

Two Make-Ahead Tips:
• You can make the batter a few hours ahead, cover with a thin layer of flour and refrigerate. Remove flour before frying.
• You can freeze latkes. They'll still taste wonderful, though not extraordinary.

This is an old family recipe (sometimes called noodle pudding, but it's not a pudding), handed down by my first husband's grandmother. It's a variation of another kugel that used to be a staple in nearly every Jewish home. The original is made with lots of cheese, sour cream, and eggs. This one keeps the eggs but eliminates the cheese and sour cream, so is somewhat heart-healthier. (Besides, now they tell us we can eat eggs again.) This dish is versatile. It can be a side dish, a main dish, or even a dessert.

BOOKS BY CLAIRE PRICE-GOFF INCLUDE:

Extraordinary Women Journalists
Twentieth Century Women Political Leaders

Kugel With Fruit

1 pound wide noodles
½ stick butter or margarine
1 can crushed pineapple, drained
4 to 5 eggs, beaten
¾ cup sugar
1 cup orange juice
½ cup raisins

Cook noodles for 10 minutes. Drain, rinse quickly. Melt butter in the same pot used for the noodles. Dump noodles into melted butter and add all other ingredients. Turn into greased 9 x 13-inch baking dish and bake at 350° F for about 60 minutes or until a butter knife comes out clean—like custard

This was my grandmother's recipe for making potato latkes. I still make them this way at Hanukkah time. The only difference is that my grandmother used schmaltz instead of vegetable oil. Shmaltz is rendered chicken fat, loaded with cholesterol, terribly bad for you, but oh so good! My grandmother would render the fat from chickens we had for dinner. She saved it in peanut butter jars in the refrigerator so there would be plenty for Hanukkah latkes. My brother and I used to sneak spoonfuls of shmaltz or smear it on bread like butter when our grandmother wasn't looking. It's a wonder we're still alive. On the other hand, my grandmother lived to be ninety-one. Maybe the secret to long life is eating lots of shmaltz and having a glass of cognac every night before going to bed.

My grandmother was a great person. Her name was Clara Kerker, but I called her Nana. She is the one who gave me a lifelong love for stories and storytelling. She is the model for Bubba Brayna in The Chanukah Guest. Hershel and the Hanukkah Goblins is dedicated to her.

BOOKS BY ERIC KIMMEL INCLUDE:

Valiant Red Rooster
The Witch's Face: A Mexican Tale
The Chanukah Guest
Hershel and the Hanukkah Goblins

Potato Latkes

This recipe uses hot oil to fry the latkes. This can cause severe burns if handled carelessly. If a child uses this recipe, always make sure an adult is present. The same is true when cooking any other fried foods.

8 medium potatoes
2 medium onions
3 large eggs
$\frac{1}{4}$ cup unbleached flour or matzo meal

$\frac{1}{4}$ teaspoon salt
$\frac{1}{8}$ teaspoon pepper
vegetable oil

Peel potatoes. If they are washed and clean, it is not necessary to peel them. Peel onions. Grate potatoes and onions using a grater, food processor, or blender. Be sure grated potatoes and onions are well-mixed together. Place mixture in a colander or sieve. Allow to drain. Place mixture in a large bowl. Add eggs, flour, salt, and pepper. Mix well with your hands to combine the ingredients.

Heat 1 inch of oil in a frying pan. Drop 1 heaping tablespoon of mixture into the pan. Each tablespoon will make one latke. Flatten with a spatula and fry for 2 to 3 minutes. When the edges turn golden brown, turn over latkes and fry on the other side for 1 to 2 minutes more. Each side should be golden and crispy. Remove latkes from the pan. Place on paper towels to drain excess oil.

Latkes are usually served with applesauce and sour cream. But you might prefer yogurt, sugar, or jam. Or just eat them plain!

My grandmother lived with us. She was born in the Ukraine and so was my mother. My grandmother, we called her Baba, was a great cook and baker, and I have always been a great eater. I used to hang around the kitchen when she baked because I loved to play with the dough, but I never learned how to cook. When I turned thirty I decided to go to cooking school for four months. Wouldn't you know it, working, not playing, with dough was my favorite, making breads, homemade pasta, pizza, and even cookies. So when I went back to work illustrating books, I wanted to try working with clay and other materials to make three-dimensional images, and I felt right at home. The only difference is that they're not edible.

BOOKS WRITTEN OR ILLUSTRATED BY LISA DESIMINI INCLUDE:

I am Running Away Today
My House
In a Circle Long Ago
Love Letters
Tulip Sees America

Pierogies

Unbleached flour, as much as needed	2 tablespoons vegetable oil (optional)
1 egg	3 cups water (lukewarm)
¼ teaspoon salt	mashed potatoes

Make a well with flour. Crack egg inside well, add salt and oil. Start mixing with your hands, adding water to make a moist dough that is not sticky. Knead dough until it is as soft as a baby's behind. Wrap it and chill it in the refrigerator for 30 minutes.

Roll it out to ¼ inch thick. Cut circles with a large glass, the size of your palm.

Fill with mashed potatoes or farmer's cheese mixed with an egg yolk. You can even use blueberries. Fold in half and pinch the half circle with your fingers to completely seal. Boil until they float, about 3 to 4 minutes. Serve with sour cream, applesauce, or mustard. Be creative.

This is the way I remember it—one evening my parents bundled my two sisters and me into the back seat of the car and drove to the airport. We arrived in time to pick up my grandfather, who had returned from a trip to Italy. With him was his new wife, our new nonna, the only grandmother we would know.

I can't remember the way she looked then—if she looked like a grandmother should look. But I do remember staying overnight in a big bed that you had to climb into and taking baths in a claw foot tub. I remember how she loved haute couture, and how my sisters and I thought we could understand everything she said, even though she spoke only Italian. And how I wished I could speak Italian, too, when we found her frightened and praying in the field after her first earthquake.

But most of all, I remember how much love can be found in a bowl of gnocchi, my nonna's gnocchi, made especially for me. That's how I remember it.

BOOKS BY PENI GRIFFIN INCLUDE:

Orange Cat Goes to Market
The Switching Well
Treasure Bird
Margo's House
A Dig in Time

My Nonna's Gnocchi

1½ pounds of potatoes   1 cup flour
1½ teaspoons salt

Boil, then finely mash the potatoes. Gently knead in the flour and salt. Form the dough into a ball. On a floured board, divide the ball into 4 equal pieces. Make a snake out of each piece. Cut each strip into 1-inch squares. Drop the squares into a pot of boiling water. When they rise to the top, boil for one more minute. Place in a serving dish and add a marinara or pesto sauce, topped with a sprinkling of Parmesan cheese.

My grandmother was known as Miz Berlin to her Hampton Road, Virginia, neighbors, but I knew her as Grandma. She let me help with the chopping and mashing part of making applesauce and left a lot in the pan for me to eat warm. When I was grown up, she had a bad fall, broke her hip, and never quite recovered. She did not know me after that and died a year later. But whenever I remember her, I remember the smell of applesauce cooking in her kitchen and the sound of my chopper inside the wooden bowl.

"GRANDMOTHER"

Time creeps down her cheeks on little crowfeet,
And birds delight in the braided nest
Of her hair. There are always pins

Falling gently on her breast
And collecting in house corners. (I would sit
On the back steps with tins

Of sardines, bowls of applesauce, a plate of meat,
And from the cellar she would bring
Canned fruit to our midday feast.)

I have watched her plump hands
Grow slow and mist slowly creep
Into her eyes. And she rests

Every afternoon while I keep
The watch instead. And now I bring
The fruits and tell the rest

Of the story; of the times
When she raised her six
And worked the store, and sleep

Was a luxury. And of the while
That she was the adult, and I the child.

BOOKS BY JANE YOLEN INCLUDE:

Water Music
Once Upon a Bedtime Story
Jane Yolen's Old MacDonald Songbook
Owl Moon

Miz Berlin's Applesauce

8 medium apples   3- inch stick cinnamon
½ to 1 cup water   ½ cup sugar

Quarter and core the apples, do not pare. Chop them in a wooden bowl with a chopper. Combine apples, water, and cinnamon in a pot. Cover and simmer until tender, about 10 to 15 minutes. Remove cinnamon.

Mash apples through a sieve, which will catch the skin and rougher parts. Stir in the sugar.

Some of my best childhood memories are of the long, lazy summer days I spent at the pond. Coming home to my mother's freshly baked blueberry pie made the day complete. Of course, the blueberries tasted especially delicious since we picked them ourselves! Nowadays my children feel that no autumn is complete unless we've spent a long, lazy day picking apples! Since we just can't decide which kind of apple is the best, I've come up with a combination applesauce—sweet and tart all at once. Of course, it is especially delicious when you pick the apples yourself!

BOOKS BY ALYSSA SATIN CAPUCILLI INCLUDE:

Peekaboo Bunny
Inside a Barn in the Country
Good Morning, Pond
Biscuit
Biscuit Finds a Friend

Everybody's Favorite Apple Applesauce

5 yellow delicious apples	generous pinch nutmeg
5 Macintosh apples	⅓ cup brown sugar
5 Granny Smith apples	½ tablespoon cinnamon
1 cup apple cider	

Peel and core apples. Cut into large chunks and place in a large saucepan. Add cider and simmer for about 30 minutes, uncovered. Stir frequently. Add nutmeg, sugar, and cinnamon. Mash apples to the desired consistency. Try substituting your own favorite apples, too.

Main Dishes

Illustration © 1987 Tedd Arnold from *No Jumping on the Bed!*, Dial Books

*W*_{hen} *I was a child, my parents did not entertain frequently, because it was wartime and my father, a career army officer, was most often overseas. But I remember occasional dinner parties, with the fancy tablecloth brought out and the silver polished and the children tucked away upstairs; in retrospect, I think they must have occurred when Dad came home on leave. For such parties my mother always cooked a chicken dish that my sister and I thought the most exotic thing we'd ever tasted (we got to eat the leftovers the next day).*

Now, reading the recipe, which my mother gave me when I grew up, I realize that it's not very exotic at all. It's easy to cook, relatively inexpensive for a large group, and it's also—I suspect now—obsolete. I haven't seen "stewing hens" in the supermarket for years. I suppose you could just use plain old chicken and cut the cooking time down to an hour.

But, hey . . . it will never be as good as it was when I was a little girl and thought my mother had a magical and glamorous touch.

BOOKS BY LOIS LOWRY INCLUDE:

A Summer to Die
Anastasia Krupnik
Rabble Starkey
Number the Stars
The Giver

Country Captain

3 stewing hens, cut up	1 box raisins
4 onions, chopped	1 cup almonds
3 green peppers, chopped	2 teaspoons curry powder
2 teaspoons thyme	3 cans tomatoes
1 cup chopped parsley	3 cloves garlic
salt and pepper	

Sauté chicken until brown and set aside. Sauté onions and peppers till softened; add other ingredients and pour over chicken in large covered casserole. Bake at 300° F about 4 hours. Serve with rice. Serves 12.

Patricia Harrison Easton

I *created this recipe to prevent resolution in my household. A book deadline was demanding long hours at my computer. Everyone was pitching in to help, but we were all getting sick of pizza. This quick and easy main dish, served with microwaved baked potatoes, corn on the cob, and slice tomatoes made all of us smile.*

BOOKS BY PATRICIA HARRISON EASTON INCLUDE:

Summer's Chance
Rebel's Choice
Stable Girl
A Week at the Fair

Deviled Chicken Breast

Preheat oven to 400° F

Mix: ½ cup Dijon mustard   3 tablespoon honey
        ⅛ to ¼ teaspoon red pepper (according to your family's
                tolerance for spicy food)

Combine: 1½ cups seasoned Italian breadcrumbs
           ⅓ cup grated Parmesan cheese
           salt and pepper to taste

Trim, rinse and pat dry:
        4 large boneless, skinless chicken breast halves

Spread the honey mustard mixture over the chicken breasts, covering thoroughly. Dip into breadcrumbs and cheese, patting lightly to get crumbs to stick. Place on an oven tray greased with oil (I use olive oil). Drizzle 2 tablespoons of the oil over the breaded chicken breasts. Bake for approximately 20 minutes or until the breasts are cooked.

When I was a kid in California in the sixties, my parents put on these great luaus for their friends. My father was an art teacher and had an excellent eye for detail. My mom was a very good cook. Between the two of them, they transformed our suburban house into a wonderful hot pink muumuu. Best of all was the dry ice my dad dropped into the backyard pond and into the punch bowl. I was fascinated by the magic of this substance that bubbled so fiercely, and terrified as well as I'd been warned consistently, "Don't touch or it will burn you." How could something cold burn me? It was a great time to be a kid, at least until bedtime.

My mom's Hawaiian drumettes are sticky and succulent. The perfect finger food that forces you to lick your fingers afterward. They are best if served with punch from a bowl with dry ice. Paper umbrellas for accompanying drinks are a must.

BOOKS BY BRUCE BALAN INCLUDE:

The Cherry Migration
Pie in the Sky
The Moose in the Dress
Jeremy Quacks

Hawaiian Drumettes

24 chicken wings or 36 drummettes	⅓ cup sugar
4 green onions	1 clove garlic, crushed
1 cup soy sauce	½-inch piece fresh ginger root,
2 tablespoon oil	crushed

Disjoint chicken wings, discarding tips. Finely chop onions, including green portion. Combine onions, soy sauce, oil, sugar, garlic, and ginger and mix well in a deep bowl. Add chicken wings and marinate at least 45 minutes, stirring occasionally. Remove chicken wings, do not drain. Place in single layer on a cookie sheet or shallow baking pan. Reserve marinade. Bake at 350° F for 15 minutes. Turn and baste with marinade. Cook 15 minutes longer.

The truth is, I rarely use recipes. My husband does our serious cooking, but my offering may strike a cord with writers and illustrators who spend more time messing up their studio than messing up the kitchen. The bottom line is I do like to eat, so...

BOOKS ILLUSTRATED BY NANCY POYDAR INCLUDE:

At the Laundromat
At the Library

Simple Roast Turkey

Get a fresh turkey and bring it to the man behind the counter. Tell him you want just the breast, hotel style, and you don't want the giblets or the neck. Ask him to put a pop-up thermometer in it. At home, preheat the oven to 350° F. Wash the turkey breast and pat it dry. Put it in a roasting pan. Slather some butter on the skin and at least pepper it. Put it in the oven. Go back to work. Enjoy the aroma wafting through the house. When you need a little break, brush the juices and melted butter in the pan over the roast. Check the pop-up thermometer. Done? Let it sit about 15 minutes (it takes that long to wash the paint off your brushes and dump the dirty water).

This can give you two or three days of just baking potatoes or preparing rice. You won't have to stop writing or painting until five or six o'clock! And think of the midday sandwiches!

I grew up in Georgia in a time when no one was health conscious. We figured out a way to fry almost everything. I still remember the huge chunk of lard we kept beside the stove for frying, the jars of bacon grease we saved in the refrigerator for seasoning, and the chunks of fat-back we threw in with the fresh vegetables to make them taste better. I wonder that my arteries weren't clogged by the time I was seven.

In those days, food was a way of life to Southerners. It was an unwritten law of Southern hospitality that guests were to be fed, no matter what time of day they dropped in. No self-respecting Southerner would be caught dead without at least one fresh homemade cake and/or pie saved back for company. My mother was a wonderful cook who particularly loved casseroles and homemade cakes.

There were so many delicious staples in the Southerner's diet— fried okra, squash and onions, cheese grits, gumbo, black-eyed peas, collard greens, butter beans, fried green tomatoes, corn bread, any number of chicken casseroles, cakes, cakes, and more cakes, and but-termilk biscuits so light they floated to the table by themselves, to name a few.

Though I eat healthier now, I still love many of these things, and once in a while I get such a hankering for something fried that there's no point in fighting it. So I indulge.

BOOKS BY HELEN KETTEMAN INCLUDE:

Bubba, the Cowboy Prince
The Christmas Blizzard
Luck With Potatoes
The Year of No More Corn

Hot Chicken Souffle

2 cups diced chicken	2 eggs
½ cup toasted pecans	1½ cups milk
¼ cup diced onion, green pepper	1 tablespoon Worcestershire sauce
½ cup diced pimientos, celery	a few drops Tabasco
½ cup mayonnaise	1 can cream of mushroom soup
4 to 6 slices bread	½ cup grated cheese

Mix chicken, pecans, onion, green pepper, pimiento, celery, and mayonnaise. Butter 2-quart casserole. Butter bread slices, remove crusts, and line bottom and sides of casserole dish (buttered side to dish). Put in chicken mixture. Beat eggs, milk, Worcestershire, and Tabasco, and pour over chicken mixture. Put in refrigerator overnight. When ready to cook, pour cream of mushroom soup over top, spread evenly, and place in 350° F oven. Cook until soup bubbles well, about 30 minutes. Remove from oven, sprinkle cheese over top, and return to oven until cheese melts.

Of all my mother's wonderful chicken casseroles, this was always my favorite. And it's convenient for company because it can be made the day ahead.

One evening in winter, when I was still living at home in Hong Kong, Mother brought home four small ducks. Each one was about two pounds. It was the only time she had bought that many, because they were on sale. Surprisingly, she cooked everybody one. She cooked them one at a time in the wok. When she finished cooking the first one, she asked, "Who wants to eat first?" We took turns eating the golden brown, garlic-flavored ducks as they were done. We didn't eat anything else, not even rice. We ate almost all the parts of the duck, including the head and the feet; we even chewed the tasty bones. The flavor stayed with us for hours. It was an unforgettable meal, because we had never eaten a whole duck each before! To tell you the truth, every time I fixed this dish for my children, it has never tasted as good as Mother's.

BOOKS BY CHING YEUNG RUSSELL INCLUDE:

First Apple
Water Ghost
Lichee Tree
Moon Festival

Garlic Duck

Recipe from my mother, Chul-Bing Chan Yeung

3 tablespoons oil
1 clove garlic, smashed
8 thin slices of ginger root, smashed
2 leeks, cut into 2-inch-long pieces
2 tablespoons soy sauce
1 teaspoon cornstarch, dissolved
   in one tablespoon tap water

1 tablespoon cooking wine
1 teaspoon sugar
1 teaspoon salt
1/4 cup water
   quartered duck (about three pounds)

Pat duck dry with a paper towel. Put oil into a wok and heat on high. When oil starts to smoke, add garlic, ginger, and leeks and quickly stir until the garlic turns golden. Then put in the duck and stir about 5 minutes, until the outside of the meat is browned. Pour in soy sauce, corn starch, wine, sugar, salt, and water. Stir well, and cover wok. Turn heat down to medium and simmer for about 15 to 20 minutes, stirring occasionally. (If there is too much water, add a little more dissolved cornstarch. About 2 tablespoons of juice is all the liquid you want when the duck is done.) Serve hot with plain, cooked rice.

BOOKS BY JONATHAN LONDON INCLUDE:

Ali, Child of the Desert
The Eyes of Grey Wolf
A Koala for Katie

Mom's (Anne London's) Spaghetti with Roast Chicken

ground beef
olive oil (splash)
tomato paste
canned whole tomatoes
4 cloves fresh garlic
splash of red wine
mushrooms (sautéed in olive oil or butter)

chopped onions
oregano
2 pinches rosemary
basil, thyme, chili pepper
MSG
pinch of sugar
salt and pepper (fresh ground)

Let simmer for 2 hours (with meat in it). Add water if too thick. Serve on fresh spaghetti with roast chicken and garlic bread. EAT!

Where I grew up, my little hometown had an Italian restaurant with the best food. Eating there with my parents was always a special treat. Maybe that's why I've always loved spaghetti. By the time I became a daddy, I could hold my own with the finest spaghetti makers, at least among fathers. My wife, Anna Grossnickle Hines, thought so, too, and wrote her book, Daddy Makes the Best Spaghetti. *To some people I appear quiet and reserved. If they only knew. Inside lurks a goofball yearning to be free. Actually, my whole family is pretty silly. Of course, what I think is goofy others may find odd, so I keep it under control. But not when I make spaghetti! The secret is in the flourish and the dancing and the flair! Also, I've never been good at reading recipes, which is why my spaghetti never tastes the same way twice. It's always a surprise.*

BOOKS BY GARY HINES INCLUDE:

A Ride in the Crummy
The Day of the High Climber
Flying Firefighters
The Christmas Tree in the White House

Daddy's Spaghetti

1 disposition: bold and free
1 pound hamburger
4 chopped celery stalks
1 small chopped onion
1 clove chopped garlic
2 16-ounce cans tomato sauce

2 16-ounce cans diced tomatoes
$\frac{1}{2}$ teaspoon Italian seasonings
$\frac{1}{2}$ teaspoon cumin
$\frac{1}{2}$ teaspoon basil leaves
$\frac{1}{2}$ teaspoon thyme leaves

Cook hamburger, celery, onion, and garlic in skillet. Drain grease. Meanwhile, heat tomato sauce and diced tomatoes in a saucepan. With flourish, add seasonings. Singing helps. Dance and prance around the room. Add contents of skillet to saucepan. Shout, "Magnifico!" Turn heat to low and let simmer for 1 hour. Add water if necessary. Serve over cooked spaghetti. As skill develops, experiment with other seasonings.

My folks weren't the best cooks when I was growing up. Mom was raising three kids in the fifties, which meant she put together the classics like tuna casserole and toasted cheese sandwiches. Dad cooked upon occasion, but it was either creamed chipped beef or pancakes. (The irony is that he's a gourmet cook now, in demand in his hometown for private dinner parties. Mom has finer taste as well.) I do remember Dad making noodles from scratch every so often. I'd watch him roll out the dough and hand cut each noodle with a long knife, laying each strand out to dry on a floured cloth. They were the best noodles in the world and probably gave me my love for pasta. I could eat pasta every single day of the week and not get tired of it. Below is my own recipe for a pasta dish I developed for another small cookbook in Connecticut (a fund raiser for the New Haven School System).

BOOKS BY DOUG CUSHMAN INCLUDE:

Camp Big Paw
Aunt Eater's Mystery Vacation

Pasta with Olives and Basil

2 tablespoons extra virgin olive oil
1 medium onion
3 to 4 cloves garlic, minced
4 Roma tomatoes, seeded and
    chopped
  about 28 Kalamata olives,
    seeded and chopped

$\frac{1}{2}$ to 1 teaspoon pepper flakes
$\frac{1}{3}$ cup fresh basil, chopped
    fresh ground pepper
1 pound angel hair pasta (or your
    best homemade pasta!)
  grated Parmesan or Romano cheese
    (I use a combination of both)

Sauté onion in oil for a minute or two over medium heat. Add garlic. Sauté for about 3 to 4 minutes, making sure garlic doesn't brown. Add tomatoes. Heat through another 3 minutes. Lower heat to medium low. Add olives and pepper flakes. Heat through, and add basil, reserving a little for garnish. Add ground pepper to taste. Turn heat to low and cover.

Cook pasta according to package directions, making sure it is al dente. Place a helping of pasta on a warm plate and top with olive and basil sauce. Sprinkle with cheese and garnish with chopped basil. Serves 2 to 3.

I *have no idea why this dish is called Spanish Spaghetti. My grand-ma Ida made it for my mother, and my mother made it for me and my two sisters. And Spanish Spaghetti is the name it came with. I do know, though, that I loved this casserole, piping hot, on a cold, snowy day in the Minnesota of my childhood. Today we would call it comfort food.*

Winters in Minnesota meant that we didn't have many fresh foods. Besides, in those years, families didn't have two cars, so my mother couldn't get to the grocery at a whim. Often she had to cook with foods on hand from the cupboard. And these spaghetti ingredients were always on hand. (So was Jell-o!)

BOOKS BY NANCY SMILER LEVINSON INCLUDE:

Christopher Columbus, Voyager to the Unknown
Turn of the Century: Our Nation 100 Years Ago,
Clara and the Bookwagon
Snowshoe Thompson
She's Been Working on the Railroad

Spanish Spaghetti

Cook: ½ pound spaghetti

Sauté: 3 cloves garlic   1 small onion, chopped
        4 celery stalks, chopped
        6 mushrooms, sliced, or small jar mushrooms

Add sautéed vegetables to drained spaghetti. Also add:

1 15-ounce can chopped tomatoes   1 teaspoon salt
   1 small can petite peas, with juice   ½ teaspoon pepper

Mix and pour into greased Pyrex or casserole dish. Bake uncovered at 350° F for about 45 minutes.

To me, spaghetti and meatballs is a very funny food—funny to say, fun to play with, fun to eat, and fun to cook. Spaghetti is an inexpensive feast. I grew up in a family of six, the second of four boys. By the time I was twelve, with both Mom and Dad working, my older brother and I had to take turns preparing dinner. At first, Mom wrote out minimal instructions or marked a page in a cookbook. As we became better cooks, she had only to list what she planned and we fixed it. Back then, spaghetti was an every-week mainstay at our house. And it still is!

BOOKS BY TEDD ARNOLD INCLUDE:

Green Wilma
No Jumping on the Bed!

Spaghetti

MEAT SAUCE:

1 large can tomatoes
1 6-ounce can tomato paste
3 tablespoons olive oil
1 medium onion, finely chopped
1 small green pepper, finely chopped, seeds removed

1 stalk celery, finely chopped, leafy portion included
½ pound lean ground beef, browned
1 bay leaf

Combine ingredients. Season to taste with salt, pepper, oregano, thyme, basil (if fresh, add during last 15 minutes of cooking).

Optional: chili powder, marjoram, cumin, cayenne, teaspoon sugar, celery seed, paprika, mild Italian sausage chopped and browned, minced carrot, flat beer (if sauce gets too thick). No two batches of my sauce are ever the same. As a kid, when Mom bought our first electric blender, we went crazy making sauce. We blended in everything, including otherwise undesirable leftovers such as succotash, Brussels sprouts, and beets.

During last 15 minutes of cooking add:

1 small can mushrooms, undrained   1 small, finely chopped onion
1 or 2 large garlic cloves, minced

Bring to boil. Reduce heat and simmer until sauce reaches desired thickness. Cover. Cook at least 1 hour, stirring regularly. When I was a kid, no one seemed to know that overcooking depleted nutrients. Our ideal cooking time for truly mellow spaghetti sauce was all-day long, or at least 4 hours, being careful to monitor thickness and not scorch the bottom of the pot. We always made meat sauce, even with meatballs.

Nothing Fancy Meatballs

1 pound lean ground beef
1 small onion, finely chopped
1 slice bread, dry or toasted, and
   crumbled fine

¼ teaspoon oregano
¼ teaspoon garlic powder
   salt and pepper to taste

Shape into 1-inch balls. Place in skillet and brown well on all sides. Drain. Add to sauce for the last half hour of cooking.

Pasta

1 pound vermicelli
4 quarts water

1 tablespoon olive oil
1 tablespoon salt or to taste

Add dry noodles to rapidly boiling water. Fork apart and stir well to prevent clumping. Return quickly to boil (or keep it boiling, if possible). Reduce heat to simmer and cook until done. I have used three ways of testing for doneness. Remove one noodle from the water and cut it in half. If you see a light spot in the center, it isn't done yet (best for fatter noodles). I learned the second method from an old TV sitcom. If you fling a noodle against the wall and it sticks, it's done. Hey, it works! The third and most reliable method is to chew a sample.

"M-m-m," said Walter, "spaghetti is my all-time favorite!" But before he could eat, his bed smashed through the table and kept right on crashing down through the floor.

Down and down fell Walter, Miss Hattie, the plate of spaghetti, the bed, and all.

M_y *mother grew up in a motherless household in Spokane, Washington, during the Depression. At a time when chow mein and spaghetti were foreign words from exotic places, she and her two sisters created a dish that combined elements of each. They called it Chinese Noodles. For my brother, sister, and me, this meal was a special treat. We always requested it for lunch on the first day of summer vacation, as well as on winter and spring breaks. As an adult, I consider Chinese Noodles a comfort food.*

BOOKS BY JANET GILL INCLUDE:

Fatal Delivery
When Darkness Calls

Chinese Noodles

1 package (1 pound) Rose Brand
  Chinese Noodles, or other thin
  noodles
ketchup

diced chicken (optional)
chopped green onions (optional)
butter or margarine

Reserve 10 to 15 noodles and boil the rest according to package directions. Break the reserved noodles into small pieces and brown in butter or margarine. Place each serving of noodles in a bowl, add some butter or margarine and stir until butter is melted. Add chicken and green onion, if desired, sprinkle fried noodles on top, and pour on ketchup to taste. Stir. Enjoy. Serves 3 or 4.

When I was twelve or thirteen, I met a woman who had recently arrived in the U.S. from China. She didn't speak much English and was having trouble meeting people, so my mother suggested that I spend an afternoon with her. As it turned out, we got along quite well, and she offered to teach me how to make won ton soup.

Basically, won tons are pork-filled dumplings that you serve in hot chicken broth. They're delicious, and I've made thousands of them over the years. They take time to prepare, however, so be patient. The trickiest part is learning to seal the won ton wrapper once the pork is inside. Don't give up—in this case, practice really does make perfect!

Won tons freeze beautifully, by the way. I always have a bag or two stashed away in my freezer. And once you've learned to make won tons, potstickers are a snap!

BOOKS BY ALAN SCHROEDER INCLUDE:

The Stone Lion
Ragtime Tumpie

Won Tons

2 to 2½ cups meat (lean pork, pork
and roast beef, pork and
crabmeat, pork and fish)
½ to 1 cup vegetables (mushrooms,
bamboo shoots, water chestnuts,
etc.)

1 scallion stalk
1 tablespoon soy sauce
½ teaspoon salt
won ton skins
egg white

Mince or grind meat and vegetables. Combine with soy sauce and salt. Mix well. Let stand for 30 minutes. Wrap mixture by large tablespoons in won ton skins, the edges of which have been dipped in egg white. Fold, sealing edges together.

Drop won tons into vigorously boiling salted water. (Add gradually so as not to disrupt boil.) Cook until they float to the top (approximately 10 minutes). Drain well.

May be added to hot chicken broth—or soup of choice—1 to 2 minutes before serving.

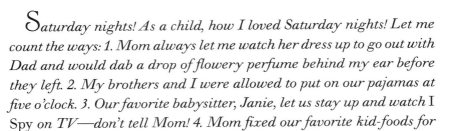

S*aturday nights! As a child, how I loved Saturday nights! Let me count the ways: 1. Mom always let me watch her dress up to go out with Dad and would dab a drop of flowery perfume behind my ear before they left. 2. My brothers and I were allowed to put on our pajamas at five o'clock. 3. Our favorite babysitter, Janie, let us stay up and watch I Spy on TV—don't tell Mom! 4. Mom fixed our favorite kid-foods for dinner: pigs-in-a-blanket, fish sticks, or macaroni and cheese. And we got to eat in our pajamas! Wow—now that was living!*

Now that I've grown up, I don't much care to pig out on pigs-in-a-blanket. And I'd swap a rubbery fish stick for a succulent steak of grilled swordfish any old day. But once in a while, on a cold Saturday night, there's nothing my husband, son, and I like better than putting on our p.j.'s, plopping down in front of the TV, and dishing up a hot and bubbly serving of macaroni and cheese. (Sometimes we even stay up till ten o'clock. Shhh—don't tell Grandma!)

BOOKS BY LEE WARDLAW INCLUDE:

Seventh-Grade Weirdo
101 Ways to Bug Your Parents
Punia and the King of Sharks
Bubblemania: A Chewy History of Bubble Gum
Bow-Wow Birthday

Really Cheesy Macaroni and Cheese

2 cups large elbow macaroni
1 cup milk*
1¼ cups grated cheddar cheese*
1¼ cups grated Swiss cheese*
2 green onions, chopped

1 green bell pepper, chopped
salt and pepper
1 large tomato, chunked
¼ cup grated Parmesan cheese

Preheat oven to 350° F.
Lightly spray nonfat cooking spray into a 1- or 2-quart casserole dish.
In a large saucepan, boil macaroni according to package directions.

*may substitute reduced fat cheese and 1% lowfat milk.

Drain in a colander, then return macaroni to saucepan. Stir in milk, making sure macaroni is completely coated. Add cheddar cheese; blend well. Add Swiss cheese and blend well. Stir in onions and bell pepper; add salt and pepper to taste. Pour mixture into casserole dish, and top with chunks of tomato. Sprinkle with Parmesan cheese and bake for 45 to 50 minutes. Feeds 4. Serve with a tossed green salad. (Apple chunks in the salad and a simple vinegar and oil dressing are a nice complement to the cheese.)

My mother loved to throw dinner parties when I was growing up. Friends would drive miles to feast on her colorful, mouth-watering Korean dishes. These dumplings were my favorite. On the day of the party, I'd rise early to watch my mother wrap the mondus, then pan-fry them on the stove. We would enjoy the most remarkable conversations as the sun rose behind us, outside the kitchen window. The memory of my mother cooking mondu is so vivid, I was inspired to write it into a scene in Tae's Sonata, *my middle-grade novel.*

BOOKS BY HAEMI BALGASSI INCLUDE:

Peace Bound Train

Tae's Sonata

Umma's Mondu (Korean Dumplings)

½ cake soft bean curd
1 pound lean ground beef
1 cup bean sprouts, cut into
  half inch pieces
2 scallions, finely chopped
2 garlic cloves, minced
1 teaspoon sesame oil
1 teaspoon soy sauce

1 egg
  salt (to taste)
1 tablespoon toasted sesame seeds
  (optional)
1 egg white
  package of won ton wrappers
  vegetable oil (enough to thinly
  cover bottom of pan)

Preheat oven to 350° F. Mix together first ten ingredients thoroughly. Form into quarter-sized meatballs and line on cookie sheet. Bake for 15 minutes. Cool.

Dip won ton wrapper edges in egg white. Place a meatball in center of each wrapper. Fold into a triangle, so edges meet. Press edges together (with the egg white acting as glue.)

Heat oil in large pan at medium heat. Fry mondus until lightly browned, about 2 minutes per side. Drain on a brown paper grocery bag. Enjoy plain or with favorite dipping sauce. (For a classic Korean soy dip, blend the following together: 5 tablespoons soy sauce, 1 tablespoon sesame oil, 1 teaspoon sugar, 1 scallion—finely chopped, 1 teaspoon toasted sesame seeds—optional).

Note: If you prefer, skip the baking step and wrap meatballs raw for steaming or boiling.

When my mother got married, she didn't even know how to boil water. She never did get the hang of cooking, so my sister and I learned to feed ourselves from an early age. The Survival Dumpling was easy, versatile and very, very filling. My mother is now 100 years old and still has her wits about her. She survived on a diet of canned macaroni, TV dinners and chocolate bars.

BOOKS BY NANCY FARMER INCLUDE:

Do You Know Me
The Ear, the Eye and the Arm
The Warm Place
Runnery Granary
A Girl Named Disaster

Survival Dumplings

One box biscuit mix (I prefer the kind where you only need to add water. Follow the directions on the box.)

FILLING 1:

Chop apples. Sprinkle with raisins. Use one handful per dumpling. Add a teaspoon of sugar and $\frac{1}{4}$ teaspoon margarine. Sprinkle with ground cinnamon and nutmeg before sealing. Serve with half-and-half.

FILLING 2:

One or two cooked sausages per dumpling.

FILLING 3:

Any interesting leftovers in the fridge. This can be stew, chili, or spaghetti sauce.

Roll out biscuit dough on a floured board. Cut into squares. Put filling on top, pull up the corners and pinch them together. Bake for however long it says on the box, usually 10 to 15 minutes in a 400° F oven.

My grandpa was from Siberia. After marrying my grandmother, they lived in Kiev until they moved to America. Grandpa liked eating pelmeni, which is a Siberian dumpling. When my brother, sister, and I visited Grandma Lazutin, she would make pelmeni, which was too foreign for us to say, so we called them Russian ravioli. We stood back until the circles of dough were ready. Armed with our spoons, we scooped the filling onto the circle. We had to scoop just the right amount so that the dough would stretch over it without tearing. The big challenge was to get the dough to stick around the edges and then stay attached where we pulled the ends together. When we were done, the counter was full of tiny flying saucers, as we called them. The fun part was plopping the ravioli into the boiling water and watching them rise to the top. When they rose, Grandma fished them out with a slotted spoon. We either ate them dipped in hot broth with vinegar or with mustard. My father passed on the recipe, and now I make pelmeni for my husband.

BOOKS BY NATASHA LAZUTIN WING INCLUDE:

Hippity Hop, Frog on Top
Jalapeño Bagels

Siberian Dumplings (Pelmeni)

| water | 1 bay leaf | pinch of salt |

FILLING:

1½ pounds lean hamburger   1 egg
1 medium onion, chopped fine   salt and pepper to taste

DOUGH:

2 cups flour   ½ to ¾ cup water
1 egg   ¼ teaspoon salt

BROTH:

2 tablespoons vinegar   ½ cup hot broth

Mix together all filling ingredients and set aside in bowl in refrigerator. In the meantime, boil water with 1 bay leaf and a pinch of salt in a big pot. Mix together ingredients for dough and knead. Dough should be stiff. Roll out dough into long rope shape. Cut into small pieces about a half inch wide.

On floured cutting board, roll out each piece into a circle. Put a dab of filling in the center of the circle. Fold dough over the meat, pinch edges, join two ends together, and pinch. It will look like a ravioli. When the water is boiling, drop in ravioli. When the ravioli floats, it is done. Serve with broth or mustard.

When I was little, my grandmother was always trying to get me to eat. My favorite food was Chinese. My poor grandmother! She didn't know how to cook Chinese food.

She did make a traditional Jewish dish called kreplak which is served in chicken soup. It is very much like a won ton. To get me to eat, my grandmother put on an academy award-winning performance every Saturday morning.

When my grandfather came back from synagogue, my grandmother would sneak down the hall and meet him at the door. She would hand him a paper bag. In the bag was a jar of her chicken soup with kreplak. In a loud voice, she would call out, "Grandpa's back with the won ton soup from the Chinese restaurant!" She would show me the jar before taking it into the kitchen.

At first, she had me fooled. When I caught on, I didn't want to ruin her fun, so I pretended that I believed I was eating won ton soup. At some point, we both knew we were pretending. We both thought it was funny. And her chicken soup with kreplak was yummy!

BOOKS BY ERICA SILVERMAN INCLUDE:

The Halloween House
On the Morn of Mayfest
Don't Fidget a Feather
Mrs. Fidget's Bicycle
Gittel's Hands

Jewish Won Tons (Kreplak)

FILLING:

1 pound ground or chopped chicken   1 onion

DOUGH:

2 eggs   1 egg white
2 cups sifted all-purpose flour   pinch salt
¼ to ½ teaspoon black pepper

Beat eggs lightly. Add flour to eggs and knead until dough is soft and stretchy. Dust a cutting board with flour and roll out dough so it is thin and even. Cut into 2-inch squares. Place 1 tablespoon filling on each square. Fold across to make triangles. Press edges together to close completely. Drop into boiling chicken soup for 15 minutes.

(If you don't want to make the dough, you can buy won ton skins from the grocery store.)

M_y *paternal grandfather emigrated to the United States from Hungary as a boy. He brought little more with him than a bundle of clothes and a few favorite family recipes. Dinner at Pa's house was always a treat for us grandchildren, particularly when he served his special stew with dumplings. After my grandfather passed away, my father continued the family tradition. In turn, he handed down the recipe to my sister and me. Stew with dumplings is still a family favorite at our house.*

BOOKS BY GAIL SAKURAI INCLUDE:

Peach Boy: A Japanese Legend
Mae Jemison: Space Scientist
Stephen Hawking: Understanding the Universe
The Liberty Bell
The Jamestown Colony

Stew With Dumplings

1 pound stew beef	1 64-ounce can tomato juice
1 tablespoon oil	16 carrots, peeled and quartered
½ teaspoon salt	4 large potatoes, peeled and quartered
¼ teaspoon pepper	1 large green pepper, cleaned and quartered
¼ teaspoon garlic salt	1 tablespoon minced parsley
½ teaspoon paprika	

Brown stew beef in oil in a large pot. Season with salt, pepper, garlic salt, and paprika. Slowly pour in tomato juice. Add vegetables and parsley. Cover and simmer for 2 hours, or until vegetables are tender.

DUMPLINGS:

2 eggs	½ teaspoon salt
1 cup milk	1 to 1½ cups flour

Beat eggs and milk in a large bowl. Stir in salt and flour until well blended. Drop large spoonfuls of batter into simmering stew. Cover and simmer for about 15 minutes. Dumplings should be cooked through, not gooey inside. Serves 6. Enjoy!

Every night when we were growing up, one of us four kids would ask that inevitable question, "What's for dinner?" Usually we were happy to learn it was something like chicken or pork chops or chili or tacos. But the nights we saw Mom slide the "red dish" into the oven, we'd groan. The red dish meant odds and ends thrown together—what Mom called Miltenberger Mush. It would be impossible to recreate the real Miltenberger Mush without that good old chipped red enamel covered dish, so the casserole recipe below will have to do. It's funny though, as much as we grumbled, all four of us have told Mom that we want that red dish someday.

BOOKS BY KIRBY MILTENBERGER LARSON INCLUDE:

Second Grade Pig Pals
Cody & Quinn, Sitting in a Tree

Miltenberger Mush

$3\frac{1}{2}$ cups uncooked egg noodles
1 can cream of mushroom soup
1 6-ounce can evaporated milk
$1\frac{1}{2}$ cups shredded cheddar cheese
2 cups diced cooked chicken or turkey

1 cup celery
$\frac{1}{4}$ cup diced green pepper
$\frac{1}{4}$ cup diced pimento
1 cup slivered blanched
    almonds, toasted

1. Cook noodles till tender and drain.
2. Combine and heat soup and milk. Add cheese, stir till melted. Stir in remaining ingredients, except the almonds.
3. Put noodles in red dish*. Top with almonds.
4. Bake at 400° F for 20 minutes.

*If you don't have a red dish, use 2-quart covered casserole

*P*ie *for supper! What a treat! When I was growing up, Welsh pasty was a favorite meal at our house. I always admired the way my mom could roll out three or four of these pies with such ease to feed the five of us kids. What a cook Mom is!*

Each time Mom made pasty, she told us how the miners' wives made individual pies for their husbands to take into the mines. Miners loved pasty—not just because of how good it is hot or cold, but also because it's wet. In the dust-filled coal mines, the men needed something wet at lunch to help get the dust out of their mouths and throat.

Pasty is now a favorite meal at my house—even though my pie crust never seems as good as my mom's—and I give my children the same history lesson about their Welsh ancestors.

BOOKS BY SUSAN CAMPBELL BARTOLETTI INCLUDE:

Growing Up in Coal Country
Dancing with Dziadziu
Silver at Night
No Man's Land
A Christmas Promise

Welsh Pasty

PIE CRUST FOR 9-INCH PIE:

2 cups flour	⅔ cup shortening
1 teaspoon salt	6 tablespoons ice water

Measure flour and salt into large bowl. Using pastry blender or fork, cut in shortening thoroughly. Sprinkle in water, 1 tablespoon at a time until all flour is moistened and dough almost cleans side of bowl. Divide dough in half. Shape half into flattened round on flour-covered board. With floured rolling pin, roll dough 2 inches larger than pie plate. (This is where Mom always says, "You can't be afraid of the dough.") Fold pastry into quarters and ease into pie plate.

After pie is filled, repeat with remaining half of dough.

PASTY FILLING:

$1\frac{1}{2}$ pounds sirloin steak, trimmed and cut into $\frac{1}{2}$-inch cubes
3 medium potatoes, peeled and sliced very thin
1 medium onion, finely chopped
2 tablespoons flour
3 tablespoons butter
    salt and pepper to taste

Layer $\frac{1}{3}$ of the steak, potatoes, onions, flour, and butter into bottom crust. Add salt and pepper to taste. Repeat layers 2 more times. Cover with top crust. Trim excess dough. (Mom always makes cinnamon-and-sugar pastry out of the pie crust trimmings.) Moisten top crust with cream. Bake at 400° F for 50 to 60 minutes. Serve with a tossed green salad.

CINNAMON-AND-SUGAR PASTRY:

Roll out excess pie crust. Sprinkle cinnamon and sugar over the dough, then roll into a crescent. Place in separate pie plate and bake alongside pasty for about 15 minutes.

I *met my husband, Carl, when I signed up to sell lushburgers for a church youth group at the county fair. He was assigned the same shift, and it was love at first bite. I was in the ninth grade; he was a mighty senior. Five years later, we married and we are still eating lushburgers and going to fairs. Because we are now vegetarians, I no longer have the original lushburger recipe—but this one tastes exactly the same and is a heart-healthy meal. Of course, the first recipe did okay in the heart department, too. We've been married for more than 40 years.*

BOOKS BY PEG KEHRET INCLUDE:

Cages
Night of Fear
Terror at the Zoo

Romantic Lushburgers

1 cup textured vegetable protein (TVP)
¾ cup boiling water
1 green pepper
1 clove garlic
1 stalk celery
1 carrot (I had to use at least one carrot, didn't I?)

1 tablespoon Worcestershire sauce
1 tablespoon sugar
1 tablespoon vinegar
⅓ cup ketchup
1 tablespoon chili powder
1 16-ounce can tomato puree or stewed tomatoes

In small bowl, combine TVP and boiling water. Set aside. Finely chop green pepper, garlic, celery, and carrot. Sauté until soft, using just enough water so the veggies don't stick. Add all other ingredients. Cook, stirring once or twice, for 20 minutes. Serve on hamburger buns or over rice.

*O*ne *of our boys was particularly fond of this recipe. Watching me make it one day, he was horrified to discover that Mom, a cook from the make-a-mess cooking school, had managed to stain the recipe card until it was almost unreadable. Fearing that the precious document was in serious jeopardy, he insisted on sitting down immediately and making a fresh copy. And so he did, with his recently learned cursive and eight year old, spelling.*

That's the card that sits in my recipe box and from which I have taken this recipe, some thirty years later. "Sweedish" Meatballs.

BOOKS BY BARBARA BRENNER INCLUDE:

The Tremendous Tree Book
On the Frontier with Mr. Audubon

Sweedish Meatballs

¾ pound very lean ground beef
¾ cup fine bread crumbs
¼ cup minced onion
¾ teaspoon cornstarch

pinch allspice
1 egg, slightly beaten
¾ cup whole milk
¾ teaspoon salt

SAUCE:

3 tablespoons flour
2 beef bouillon cubes
¼ cup safflower or canola oil
2 cups water

1 cup cooking burgundy for
flavor (Alcoholic content
evaporates with cooking.)

Mix meat, bread crumbs, onion, cornstarch, and all other ingredients except those under sauce. Form into meatballs about 1½ inches in diameter and brown in oil in large skillet. Remove meatballs from skillet and mix remaining oil (add a little if necessary) with flour. Add salt, bouillon cubes dissolved in boiling water, and wine, scraping pan bottom and stirring until thickened. Remove to a pot and add meatballs. Simmer uncovered for 30 minutes. Serve on brown rice or noodles. Serves 4. This recipe can be doubled nicely for a dinner party and can be made a day in advance. It doesn't freeze well.

B*oth of our mothers are excellent cooks. Our Jumpin' Ratatouille is our own concoction that is a tribute to the creative spirit that our moms brought to cooking when we were children. It's a great dish at any time of year.*

BOOKS BY ANDREA AND BRIAN PINKNEY INCLUDE:

Dear Benjamin Banneker
Seven Candles for Kwanzaa

Jumpin' Ratatouille

6 large zucchini, sliced into coin shapes*
1 clove garlic, chopped
1 medium to large onion, chopped
½ large yellow pepper, julienne
½ large red pepper, julienne
2 chives, chopped
2 26-ounce boxes crushed tomatoes
½ 6-ounce can tomato paste
½ jar salsa sauce (mild)
1 small bay leaf
¼ teaspoon cayenne pepper
½ teaspoon curry powder (reduce or add as preferred)
1 teaspoon Old Bay seasoning
2 tablespoons oregano
1 teaspoon freshly chopped basil
½ teaspoon salt (as desired)

1. Slice zucchini. Chop garlic, onion, peppers, chives.
2. Place zucchini slices in large stew pot. Fill pot with cold water, enough to cover zucchini. Bring pot to a steady boil. Let boil until zucchini is moderately tender, not soft. Pour off all water, using a strainer. Return zucchini to pot.
3. Add crushed tomatoes, onion, peppers, and chives to zucchini.
4. Bring pot to a vigorous boil. Let boil for 5 minutes, then reduce heat to a slow, rolling boil. Let boil this way for up to 10 minutes, stirring occasionally to reduce chance of sticking. Using tilted pot lid to catch solid ingredients, drain off all watery tomato broth from mixture, leaving zucchini, tomato chunks, peppers, onions.

---

*Yellow summer squash works also. For variety, you can make this recipe with 3 zucchini and 3 summer squash

5. Return pot to stove. Add salsa sauce, tomato paste, garlic, and bay leaf. Stir. Bring to a boil, then reduce to simmering.
6. Add cayenne pepper, curry powder, Old Bay seasoning, oregano, basil, salt. Stir.
7. Let simmer on low heat for 20 minutes, stirring occasionally. Mixture should be like a thick, chunky stew.
8. Let mixture stand for 1 to 2 hours before serving to allow ingredients to soak in all flavors. Makes 6 to 8 servings.

Serving suggestions:
- Serve as a side dish, with a main course
- Serve cold or at room temperature as a party relish
- Serve as a vegetarian main dish by serving over brown rice. Sprinkle grated cheese (mozzarella, cheddar, Monterey Jack). Let cheese melt on top. Add one dollop plain yogurt. Sprinkle with dried or freshly chopped scallions.

Serve a side salad to round out the meal.

M*y mother is a remarkable woman and the only person I could ever imagine calling my hero. Raising my brother and me by herself for so many years was no easy chore—my brother is almost as big as I am! Through the hard times she never let on that money was tight, managing to be both frugal and creative with her cooking. One-dish meals were a large part of our life, and all the better if they could be stretched over several days, hence the metamorphosis of Red Beans and Rice into chili, a necessity that has become a tradition in our family.*

BOOK BY WALTER MAYES AND VALERIE LEWIS:

Walter and Valerie's Best Books for Kids: A Lively and Highly Opinionated Guide

How Do You Feed a Hungry Giant, or Kay's (Mother of Giants) Chili

1 pound red kidney beans (soak overnight & drain)
8 to 10 cups water
2 onions, quartered
1 to 2 stalks celery with leaves
1 to 3 cloves garlic, chopped

2 ham hocks or ½ pound ham slice
1 large bay leaf
salt and pepper to taste
1 small can tomato sauce

Boil beans with all above ingredients (except tomato sauce) gently for about 90 minutes, or until tender but still firm. Stir occasionally. Remove ham hocks, if used. Cool, cut meat from bone, and return bite-sized meat to beans. Add tomato sauce.

At this point, you have the bean portion of New Orleans Red Beans and Rice, which can be simmered a bit longer, so the tomato sauce flavors the beans. Serve over steamed rice.

For chili, proceed with the following. (Though it is best to refrigerate the beans and wait a day, it is not necessary.)

1 pound coarsely ground (lean) beef

1 large onion, chopped

$\frac{1}{2}$ green pepper, chopped

1 to 2 cloves garlic, chopped and salted to taste

$\frac{1}{2}$ to 1 teaspoon cumin

$\frac{1}{2}$ to 1 + tablespoon chili powder

1 to 2 teaspoons white vinegar

Brown beef, onions, green pepper, and garlic with salt and pepper. Add mixture to beans and bring to a boil. Immediately reduce heat and add cumin, chili powder, and vinegar to suit your taste buds. Cover and gently simmer for 30 minutes or so. If you like more of a tomato flavor, add stewed tomatoes before simmering.

A shortcut is to use canned kidney beans, but be sure there is no sugar added. Doctor these with whatever ingredients are needed to get rid of the canned taste. Short method or long, flavors mingle nicely overnight in the refrigerator.

The Mayes tradition is to serve over spaghetti. We understand that this practice is not observed in some parts of the country. Pity.

❧·❧· Linda Gramatky Smith ·❧·❧
In honor of Hardie Gramatky

M*y father, Hardie Gramatky, wrote and illustrated* Little Toot *back in 1939, and he would be amazed that it is still in hardcover and paperback some 58 years later! Dad died in 1979, but my mother (her nickname is "Doppy") is still doing well. A few years after* Little Toot *was published, Mom, Dad, and I (born in the interim) moved out to Westport, Connecticut, to the same house in which my husband and I now live. A couple of years later two other artists (one was Stevan Dohanos of* Saturday Evening Post *covers fame) and Dad started the Fairfield Watercolor Group. It has met continuously for 49 years. Twelve artists, who often did commercial illustrations to pay the bills, met monthly in each other's homes, bringing with them a fine art painting that they wouldn't have painted otherwise. The members of the group critiqued each work (very lovingly and gently, but with some excellent ideas of how to make it better), and the wives or husbands made comments as well. Many fine-arts careers were started from this encouragement to paint for fun. When the show and tell was done, the wives (remember, this was the 50s) would put on a great spread. And I remember how everyone talked about my mother's chili and popovers! Dad would often choose a winter month to have his turn at hosting, just so Mom could make his favorite meal!*

Doppy's Chili for a Crowd, in memory of Hardie Gramatky

2 onions, chopped
1½ pounds lean beef
1 can tomato soup, undiluted
1 can kidney beans, drained
1 can whole tomatoes, broken
   quarters (optional)
1 green pepper, chopped

1 dash of Tabasco
2 teaspoons cumin
  parsley, chopped
  salt to taste
  chili powder (at least 1 tablespoon,
   but I'd use more)

Brown onions a bit and then add meat. (Be sure not to brown meat too much—just enough to get the fat out, but with some pink, because it will cook more as the chili cooks.) Add soup, beans, tomatoes, green pepper and spices. Simmer about 90 minutes, stirring occasionally. Add more spices if desired. Good with popovers and a tossed salad! (Back in the 50s and 60s, of course, lean beef would have been used. Nowadays, this recipe tastes great made with half or more ground turkey, but make it whatever way you wish.)

No-Fail Popovers

2 eggs	1 cup milk
1 cup flour	1 teaspoon salt

Grease and flour muffin tins (10 large). Mix together ingredients, but don't worry about lumps! Fill muffin tins ¾ full. Put on cookie sheet (to prevent drips) and put in cold oven! (This is one secret of success.) Bake 30 minutes in 450° F oven. Don't peek until time's up. Stick knife in top of popovers to allow hot air to leave and then leave in oven for 5 minutes with door closed. Keep the second helpings in oven. Does anyone make popovers anymore? They are very light and puff up way above the muffin tin, with just air inside. Yields 3 to 4 servings.

Leftover chili was my absolute favorite breakfast when I was growing up. I loved it with a big glass of cold milk. I gather from the heavily stained index card from which I copied this that it was my mother's recipe originally, although I think of it as my mother's and my father's, since both of them made it regularly—and I learned to make it, too, when I was quite young. Truth be told, the chili I grew up with was even milder than this version: no chili powder, garlic or green peppers. I've tried variations of this recipe, my favorite being strictly vegetarian, in which you replace the meat with an extra can of beans and any vegetables that strike your fancy. My father, who never wanted to waste food, tried many variations, too, but most of these—involving throwing in whatever other leftovers he found in the refrigerator—were not always as successful as the original!

BOOKS BY JAMES HOWE INCLUDE:

I Wish I Were a Butterfly
The Watcher

Sebastian Barth Mysteries series
Bunnicula (vampire rabbit) series

Breakfast, Lunch and Dinner Chili

2 large onions, chopped
1 large green pepper, chopped
2 to 3 cloves of garlic, minced
1 pound ground beef

chili powder, salt, and pepper to
  taste
1 large can of whole tomatoes
1 can of kidney beans
¾ cup of rice

In a large deep-dish skillet or heavy pot, fry chopped onions in oil on medium heat. When the onions begin to soften, add peppers and garlic. Fry until the onions are yellowish. Add ground beef, turning it until there is no more red. At any point, add the seasoning (the more chili powder, the hotter the chili). Add tomatoes, with juice, and let simmer for 5 to 10 minutes. Add beans and rice and cook until rice is tender. If you want a more tomato-y chili, add some cut up fresh tomatoes, another small can of tomatoes, or juice. You may wish to serve with diced fresh onion and/or grated cheddar cheese to sprinkle on top. This is delicious heated as a leftover and served for breakfast, lunch, dinner, or anytime in-between!

My mother was a good mom but a terrible cook. I don't know if I ate like a bird because of her disastrous cooking or because by nature I was a picky eater. I have many memories of culinary disasters in our household of two adults and nine children. One Thanksgiving, my mother forgot to turn on the oven, so instead of eating roast turkey, we had to order in pizzas. On another occasion, the kitchen caught fire because my mother left bacon cooking on the stove while rescuing our gerbil from the neighbor's roof. As an adult, I've developed a huge appetite and a love for good food. The recipe below is a favorite with my children.

BOOKS BY MARGERY CUYLER INCLUDE:

That's Good! That's Bad!
Weird Wolf
Invisible in the Third Grade
Fat Santa

Hamburger-Tortilla Casserole

1 cup chopped onion
1½ to 2 pounds hamburger
1½ teaspoons cumin
2 crushed cloves garlic
1½ teaspoons chili powder
½ teaspoon pepper

1 cup water
1 large jar medium salsa
    flat corn tortillas
1 pound shredded Monterey Jack
    cheese
1 cup sour cream

Sauté onion, add beef, and brown. Drain. Add next 6 ingredients. Simmer 10 minutes until most of liquid evaporates. Pour ½ cup sauce in greased 9 x 13-inch pan. Arrange half of tortillas over sauce (cover bottom of pan). Add ½ cup sauce, beef mix, and salsa. Top with sour cream, ½ cheese, remaining tortillas, and remaining cheese. Bake uncovered 40 minutes at 375° F, uncovered for 5 minutes. Serve with guacamole, chopped tomatoes, and pitted olives on side. Serves 6.

This was the first dinner my wife ever made for me.

BOOKS BY MATT CHRISTOPHER INCLUDE:

Beloved St. Anne
Dog That Pitched a No-Hitter
Wingman on Ice

Beef Stroganoff

2-pound round steak
4 tablespoons margarine or shortening
1 clove garlic minced
1 12½-ounce can of sliced
    mushrooms with juice (2½ ounces)

1 envelope of onion soup
    mix
1¼ cups of water
2 tablespoons of flour
1 cup of sour cream

Trim fat and cut across grain of meat in thin strips. Brown meat in shortening until it loses its red color with garlic. Add mushrooms and soup mix, plus water. Stir well. Blend flour with sour cream and add to meat mixture. Put in greased casserole and bake for 2 to 2½ hours at 300° F, covered. Serve over rice or noodles. Makes 4 to 5 servings.

Members of my family always got to choose the dinner menu on their birthdays, from entree to dessert. My two younger sisters, Val and Cindy, well knew how much I loved steak, so they always hoped I'd ask Mother to cook it on my birthday. Imagine their disgust when, one year, I decided I wanted my next to favorite meal for my birthday dinner: beef hash. I remember my sisters wailing, "But that's leftovers!" My chocolate/orange marble birthday cake did nothing to placate them. They reminded me of my deed for months afterward.

Today I add mushrooms sautéed in butter, chopped green onions, and lemon juice to the old family recipe. Talk about salivating . . .

BOOKS BY MARY WHITTINGTON INCLUDE:

The Patchwork Lady
Winter's Child

Simple Fare But Best Roast Beef Hash

(The following measurements are approximate.)
½ large onion, chopped
1 to 2 tablespoons butter, margarine, or vegetable oil
2 cups leftover roast beef, cut in ½-inch cubes
2 or 3 large russet potatoes, baked, peeled, then cut in ½-inch cubes
juice from the roast, enough to moisten ingredients

Melt butter or margarine, or spoon oil into frying pan. Sauté onions till clear. Dump in meat and potatoes. Fry mixture until the aroma sets salivary glands working. Add a little meat juice just to moisten (no swimming of ingredients allowed). After about 15 minutes, transfer contents of pan to a 2 quart (at least) casserole. Can make recipe ahead of time—tastes even better that way. Reheat in oven or microwave. Or eat with fork directly from frying pan, ignoring the clamoring of family and friends. Serves 1 to 4 (or more, depending on size of recipe). Serve hash with lots of fresh corn on the cob.

*W*hen my mother asked what I would like for dinner on my four-teenth birthday I requested pork chops and beans, a family favorite. While Mom was browning the meat, my grandfather called and asked me to come to his house because he had a present for me. Dad volunteered to drive me. We were gone for about thirty minutes. When we got home a dozen of my friends jumped out from behind the furniture and yelled surprise! The dining room table was set with hot dogs, chips, and a birthday cake. Balloons and wrapped packages were scattered all over the room. We had a wonderful time at my party, but I never did figure out what happened to those pork chops.

BOOKS BY CARMEN BREDESON INCLUDE:

The Spindletop Gusher
Battle of the Alamo
American Writers of the 20th Century
Presidential Medal of Freedom Winners
Texas: Celebrate the States

Pork Chops and Beans

6 to 8 pork chops
2 28-ounce cans of pork and
   beans
$\frac{1}{4}$ cup ketchup
1 tablespoon mustard

2 tablespoons brown sugar
$\frac{1}{4}$ cup chopped onion
$\frac{1}{4}$ cup chopped green pepper
salt, pepper, celery salt, garlic salt

Brown pork chops in a skillet. In a shallow casserole dish, mix beans, ketchup, mustard, brown sugar, onion, and green pepper. Arrange pork chops over beans and spoon a little sauce over each one. Sprinkle chops with salt, pepper, celery, and garlic salt. Bake, uncovered, for 80 minutes at 350° F.

Both of my parents grew up during the Depression. They were recyclers before it became fashionable—wooden crates into end tables; scraps of material into doll dresses; plastic bleach bottles into toy cradles; leftovers into hearty meals.

Give my mother a cup of fish flakes, some cold mashed potatoes and, like magic, she'd fix my favorite Friday night dish: Angela's Friday Night Fish Cakes.

BOOKS BY EILEEN SPINELLI INCLUDE:

Where Is the Night Train Going?
Lizzie Logan Wears Purple Sunglasses
Boy, Can He Dance!

Angela's Friday Night Fish Cakes

1 cup flaked fish (cooked)
1 tablespoon chopped onion
1 teaspoon lemon juice
¼ teaspoon salt
1 tablespoon minced parsley

1 slightly beaten egg
1 cup leftover (cold) mashed potatoes
2 tablespoons flour
¼ cup vegetable oil (for frying)

Mix together fish, onion, lemon juice, salt, parsley, egg, and potatoes. Form into four patties. Coat with flour. Sauté in oil for 5 or 6 minutes. Turn once during cooking. Drain on paper towels.

Finish off the meal with a topping of stewed tomatoes and a side dish of macaroni and cheese. Yum!

Maryann Cocca-Leffler

As a child, having baked stuffed clams for dinner was a summer tradition. Our summer home is on the coast of New England. My family and I spent many mornings digging for clams with our grandfather. After he cleaned the clams and gathered the meat, we washed out the shells. Later, my mom and aunt would prepare baked stuffed clams for dinner with the recipe below. As with all Italian cooks, they never measured anything . . . so feel free to make this recipe your own by adding more breadcrumbs or more garlic or whatever. Enjoy!

This childhood memory inspired me to write Clams All Year. Through the text and illustrations I share my experience of spending summers on the shore of New England with my large extended family . . . digging lots of clams.

BOOKS WRITTEN OR ILLUSTRATED BY
MARYANN COCCA-LEFFLER INCLUDE:

Clams All Year
Missing: One Stuffed Rabbit
My Backpack
Wanda's Rose

Baked Stuffed Clams

1 pound fresh minced clam meat
2 cups bread crumbs
1/3 cup grated Romano cheese
1/3 cup butter (melted) or olive oil
1/8 cup fresh chopped parsley

1 tablespoon lemon juice
1/2 teaspoon minced garlic
1 egg
black pepper to taste
pinch of oregano (optional)

In a large bowl mix all the ingredients together except for minced clams. When thoroughly mixed, add in clams. Fill clean, dry clam half-shells* with the clam mixture. Place on a cookie sheet. Sprinkle with olive oil and bake at 400° F until brown (about 20 minutes). Serve with a lemon wedge.

*If you don't have clam shells, spread the mixture in a shallow baking dish and bake until brown.

In my family, women divided themselves into cleaners and cooks. My mom kept the most tidy and graceful house, and her sister was more carefree but could cook up a storm. Yet this dinner that my mother liked to make was always a crowd pleaser and is my favorite comfort-food meal.

Although my mother gets credit for it, I suspect that the one who taught her how to make it was my father. He falls into the cook category, too. He learned how to experiment in the kitchen by cooking with his beloved grandmother. My great-grandmother's cooking was plain but plentiful. This zesty dish benefits from her touch and my father's experimenting, but my mother served it with such grace and love that in my heart it truly belongs to her.

BOOKS BY JOANNE RYDER INCLUDE:

The Snail's Spell
Chipmunk Song
Earthdance
My Father's Hands
Where Butterflies Grow

My Mom's Zesty Pot Roast

$3^{1}/_{2}$ to 4 pound eye round or bottom round
   mustard (My mom prefers Gulden's spicy brown mustard)
2 tablespoons shortening (My mom uses Crisco; I use liquid shortening)
1 tablespoon (approximate) seasoning and browning sauce
1 large onion, cut in half
3 or 4 bay leaves

5 or 6 peppercorns
1 can condensed beef broth
5 or 6 cloves
6 medium-sized carrots, cut in half, and each half quartered lengthwise
1 to 2 tablespoons cornstarch to thicken gravy
1 large package wide egg noodles, or noodles of your choice

METHOD:

1. Heat shortening in a heavy Dutch oven with a tight-fitting lid. Cook on top of stove.
2. Lightly spread mustard on all sides of meat.
3. Brown meat well on all sides in the hot shortening.
4. When nearly brown, coat meat with Gravy Master, using pastry brush.
5. Add ½ large onion and continue browning meat and onion until onion is brown but not burnt.
6. Add beef broth, bay leaves, cloves, peppercorns, and the other half of the onion. Cover and simmer 30 minutes.
7. After the 30 minutes, check and add enough water to cover ¾ of the meat. Cover and simmer for 2 hours, occasionally turning the meat to keep it from sticking.
8. Add carrots, cover, and continue to simmer until carrots are tender—about 30 minutes. (Total cooking time is about 3 hours.)
9. When done, remove carrots and meat, strain gravy, skim off fat, and thicken gravy with cornstarch in a little cold water.
10. Cook noodles according to package directions.
11. Slice meat and serve with the carrots and noodles.

Sorry, I don't know a recipe from a receipt. Can't cook!

BOOKS BY SID FLEISCHMAN INCLUDE:

The Whipping Boy
The Scarebird
Jim Ugly

Variations on Marinades

*In honor of Sid Fleischman, because he adds so much flavor
to children's literature*

MARINADE 1:
  1 tablespoon salad oil
  ½ cup soy sauce
  ¼ cup sugar
  2 tablespoons sherry
  1 teaspoon ginger
  1 clove garlic, crushed

MARINADE 2:
  ½ cup salad oil
  ¼ cup soy sauce
  ½ cup red wine
  2 tablespoons powdered ginger
  1 clove garlic, crushed
  2 tablespoons ketchup
  ½ teaspoon pepper
  5 shakes Worcestershire sauce

MARINADE 3:
  1 cup salad oil
  ¾ cup soy sauce
  ½ cup lemon juice
  ¼ cup prepared mustard
  1 tablespoon coarsely ground
    fresh pepper
  2 cloves garlic, crushed
  ½ onion, minced

MARINADE 4:
  1 cup ketchup
  1 cup water
  2 teaspoons salt
  2 tablespoons Worcestershire
    sauce
  ½ cup vinegar
  ¼ cup brown sugar
  2 teaspoons dry mustard

MARINADE 5:
  2 cloves garlic, crushed
  1 teaspoon salt
  ½ cup chili sauce
  1 tablespoon Worcestershire
    sauce
  ¼ green pepper put through
    garlic press
  Tabasco to taste

MARINADE 6:
  ½ cup red wine vinegar
  2 tablespoons olive oil
  1 tablespoon coarse ground
    mustard
  1 clove garlic, crushed
  ½ teaspoon pepper
  ½ teaspoon sugar

BARBECUE 1:

½ cup prepared barbecue sauce

1 tablespoon Worcestershire sauce

1 clove garlic, crushed

¼ teaspoon thyme

¼ teaspoon basil

¼ teaspoon oregano

BARBECUE 2:

4 tablespoons molasses

4 tablespoons prepared mustard

3 tablespoons lemon juice

3 tablespoons soy sauce

2 tablespoons Worcestershire sauce

BARBECUE 3:

1 cup onions, chopped

½ cup ketchup

¼ cup Worcestershire sauce

⅛ teaspoon Tabasco

2 tablespoons brown sugar

1 cup vinegar

SWEET-AND-SOUR SAUCE:

3 tablespoons cornstarch

1 tablespoon soy sauce

3 tablespoons water

1 cup pineapple juice

3 tablespoons vinegar

½ cup brown sugar

Cook till thickened. Add pineapple and bell pepper chunks, if desired.

LAMB MARINADE:

½ teaspoon salt

½ teaspoon freshly ground pepper

1½ tablespoons minced parsley

1 small bay leaf

1 clove garlic, split

⅓ cup olive oil

¼ teaspoon (1 teaspoon fresh) thyme

1 cup burgundy

oregano, rosemary

BASTING BUTTER FOR FISH:

Cream ¼ cup butter till fluffy

Blend in:

1 teaspoon lemon juice

1 tablespoon finely minced: chives, thyme, rosemary, basil, tarragon, or any combination.

COATING FOR MEAT:

2 teaspoons dried thyme

4 crumbled bay leaves

1 teaspoon fennel seeds (optional)

1 teaspoon rosemary

Crush the above to powder.

Mix with:

¼ cup sour cream

3 tablespoons Dijon mustard

Coat meat. Refrigerate 24 hours, then grill.

*T*his recipe is my all-time favorite way of eating peas—or at least it's the closest I can come to the dish Grammy Barb made when I was growing up in Maine. She used to throw all sorts of interesting stuff into pots and pans and make up funny names for the results, but it was always delicious!

*W*ARNING: Grammy Barb's Rainy-Day Salmon Pea Wiggle is not for the dainty or squeamish. It smells fishy and looks like … goop! But you'll enjoy it if you're the type of person who loves going barefoot in warm mud or gets a kick out of telling your friend the grape you just peeled is an eyeball—right before you pop it in your mouth.

BOOKS BY LISA ROWE FRAUSTINO INCLUDE:

Grass and Sky

Ash: A Novel

Family Secrets (Editor and Contributor),
anthology of young adult short stories

Grammy Barb's Rainy-Day Salmon Pea Wiggle

1 big can of salmon
1 16-ounce bag of frozen peas
1 batch of plain white sauce
   (that's somebody else's recipe)

salt and pepper to taste
1 tube of plain crackers

Make the white sauce in a 2-quart saucepan. Dump in the salmon and the defrosted peas. Stir it up with salt and pepper until it's hot. Serve in big messy spoonfuls over crackers.

BOOKS ILLUSTRATED BY ED YOUNG INCLUDE:

Lon Po Po: A Red Riding Hood Story from China
Little Plum
The Other Bone
Seven Blind Mice

Rawfish Gruel

'Tis my father's Sunday special treat.

Line a bowl with fresh, thinly sliced fish, uncooked. Add a spoonful of tamari and a touch of sesame oil. Sprinkle an inch of chopped scallion. Mix in 1 fresh egg (in my case, from my brother's little hen). Stir in piping, boiling gruel of rice, and top with crisp oil-fried sticks.

My father was king of the backyard grill. When it came to cooking indoors, I never saw him make anything more than a cold sandwich, which he then ate standing up over the kitchen sink. But in the backyard, hovering over his homemade fifty-five-gallon-drum grill, he was transformed into a culinary tyrant. My younger brother, Pete, and I were his minions. He was a great cook, but we were more fascinated with the fire than the food. My father knew this, so he would work us into shape with a battery of grilling questions.

"Who invented the charcoal briquette?" he barked.

"Henry Ford," we replied.

"Do you cook fish with the grill top up or down?"

"Down," we'd sing.

"Do you ever put honey in barbecue sauce?"

We made stinky faces. "Never. Sweet sauces are for whimps."

"What do real grill men eat?" he'd ask.

"Food so hot it makes you cry," we'd reply on queue.

My father had no interest in being environmentally correct. Once he formed the briquettes into a pyramid in the bottom of the grill, he'd squirt on a pint of charcoal starter. It smelled like kerosene, and when he lit it a ball of flame whooshed up like a mini nuclear explosion. Pete and I cheered. Then, when Dad was in the house getting his tools prepared, Pete and I went to work. While the flames leapt three feet above the rim of the grill, we'd melt plastic army men, farm animals, military vehicles, airplanes and anything else we could, then arrange them in a mock town that had been hit with an atomic bomb blast.

By the time Dad returned with his plates of foods, bowls of sauces, brushes, tongs, forks of various length, a big sharp knife, and a beer, we knew he was ready to cook. And we were ready to eat.

BOOKS BY JACK GANTOS INCLUDE:

Not So Rotten Ralph
Rotten Ralph's Show and Tell

Grilled Kingfish

2 pounds kingfish fillets, cut into 8-ounce portions
lime juice (about three limes)

vegetable oil
salt
cracked black pepper to taste

Marinate the fish with lime juice in a shallow dish for 4 hours. Pat dry and brush with oil, then salt and pepper. It is important to cook the fish skin side down. Close the top of the grill for 5 to 8 minutes, then flip and cook for another 5 minutes (top down), or until done. Properly cooked, the fish should be white and juicy throughout. Do not overcook, or kingfish binds up.

FOR A SAUCE, TRY:

1 ripe mango, diced
2 tablespoons chopped cilantro
1 onion, diced

2 jalapeño chili peppers, diced
1 dash of balsamic vinegar
salt and pepper to taste

W*hen I was growing up in Iowa in the 40s, we always opened our presents on Christmas Eve. No Christmas morning see-what-Santa-brought bonanza for us. Christmas Day was reserved for church and the big Christmas dinner at our house featuring all the relatives, while Christmas Eve was our special family time of giving and sharing.*

Being Roman Catholic in those days meant no meat on Christmas Eve, just like on Fridays, so Dad always made his famous oyster stew, Mama baked homemade bread, and we had dinner in the dining room by candlelight. Then, while my sister and I placed the lantern in the window to guide the Christ child through the dark streets, Dad checked the turkey one more time for pinfeathers and Mama made her corn bread stuffing.

At nine o'clock we opened our gifts. All the lights in the house were turned off, except for those on the tree as, with great ceremony, we took turns unwrapping our presents. Dad's oyster stew always brings back those memories of love and warmth. Maybe it will be comfort food for you, too.

BOOKS BY BEBE FAAS RICE INCLUDE:

Music From the Dead
The Listeners
Love You to Death
Class Trip
The Year the Wolves Came

Dad's Christmas Eve Oyster Stew

1 pint oysters
3 tablespoons butter or margarine
4 cups milk, scalded

salt and pepper to taste
paprika

Place oysters in saucepan and barely cover with water. Simmer until edges curl. Pour in scalded milk. Add butter. Warm thoroughly. Season with salt and pepper and serve with a dash of paprika. Serves 4.

My mother was a wonderful person, but not a wonderful cook. There were numerous reasons for this, but the two main ones were as follows:

1. She simply didn't know how to cook. She could start with vegetables of any color—red beets, orange carrots, yellow corn, and green beans, but by the time she'd finished boiling the life out of them, they were a uniform gray, indistinguishable from one another.

2. She was forgetful. For example, she once left a meat loaf in the oven for an extra four hours, making it even more unpalatable than it would normally have been. This was such a momentous and unforgettable calamity that I based a poem on the event. Indeed, I can trace the origins of many of my food poems to her culinary art.

By the way, her meat loaf (except for that one) was one of my favorite dishes, right up there with her notorious burnt macaroni and cheese and her fabulous overcooked, underseasoned goulash. There really is no accounting for taste.

With all this in mind, I have submitted one of my own recipes, simple and relatively healthful, especially if you use low-fat mayonnaise. It has the further advantage of needing no cooking.

BOOKS BY JACK PRELUTSKY INCLUDE:

The New Kid on the Block
Something Big Has Been Here
The Dragons Are Singing Tonight
A Pizza the Size of the Sun
Monday's Troll

Loony Tuna

1 can tuna, drained
1 stalk celery, diced
1 stalk green onion, chopped
1 apple, cored and diced
⅓ cup raisins

1 to 2 tablespoons mayonnaise—
  just enough to moisten
a sprinkle of fresh grated black
  pepper

Mix all ingredients and serve on lettuce or toast.

Now this is a recipe handed down, mon cher. You treat it with true respect, honneur, and most sincerely amour. No one in our family knows the true origin of this tasty dish, mayhaps it came from an alligator hunter who brewed it up for good luck while he pushed his pirogue along the winding Atchafalaya. Could be it came from the granny midwife who lived in a house on stilts in the very middle of the Pascagoula. My uncle, he always claimed that his was first made by a waiter at one of the waterfront cafes in New Orleans. It was a special dish, only for riverboat captains. Qu'est-ce que Ça? *Whostosay?*

I think a lonely maman wanted to gather up everyone in her family, so she got out her big cast-iron kettle, put extra wood in the oven, and started dreaming about her children and their children and how much she wanted them to come visit her. So she started out with shrimp because her oldest daughter loved shrimp. Next it was crab, her son's special favorite. The okra was for Grandma. The tomatoes for her husband. The rice for the petite bebes. And spices, lots of spices to keep the conversation going. But sacre b/leu, it would take way too long to cook each item separately, and besides she had only one pot! Only one thing to do—gumbo.

So now, when I feel lonely for my family I make gumbo. I make it extra spicy to honor the alligator hunter, and I put in plenty of filé for the midwife, and I say blessings over it for the waiter and the riverboat captains. And mon cher, I stir it only with a wooden spoon so as not to bruise the many kisses I blow into the pot.

BOOKS BY KATHI APPELT INCLUDE:

Elephants Aloft
Bayou Lullaby
Thunderherd

My favorite meal from 1955 until 1959 was Franco-American Spaghetti with Sliced Wieners. It came in a can. It was an early version of Spaghetti-Os, with straight noodles instead of O-shaped noodles and bright orange sauce. It was as delicious as it was quick, and the recipe is right in the title.

Bon Appétit!

BOOKS BY PEGGY RATHMAN INCLUDE:

Goodnight , Gorilla
Ruby the Copycat

W*e were touring California by car with French friends, Jean-Marie and Aglaë Chance, spending every other day or so in a rented cottage in order to cook some of our meals. All four of us, my husband and I and the Chances, love to eat, but Jean-Marie is the greatest gourmand I've ever known. Remember how Donald Duck's uncle would get dollar signs in his eyes? Jean-Marie gets a knife-and-fork sign in his eyes when he sees rabbits, hares, blackbirds—and he marvels that Americans coexist so generously with these creatures by not eating them. Hiking in a beautiful valley in the eastern sierras, Jean-Marie spotted wild mushrooms and identified them by their Latin names with authority, delicately feeling under their hoods. This made me a tiny bit nervous. We all have heard the stories of people who die from eating wild mushrooms. That night, Aglaë served a delicious pork tenderloin—with mushrooms. Were they the wild ones? I'll never know, but I promise the meal was delicious. Serve the pork and its sauce over pasta, with a green salad.*

BOOKS BY SUSAN PATRON INCLUDE:

The *Billy Que* series
Maybe Yes, Maybe No, Maybe Maybe
Dark Cloud Strong Breeze

Aglae's Pork Tenderloin

Remove the tendons from a pork tenderloin. Cut it into 2-inch chunks. Melt a tablespoon each of butter and good olive oil in a casserole dish. Brown a handful or more of chopped (cultivated) mushrooms over medium high heat and set aside. Sauté a sliced onion until tender and translucent, and a clove or two of garlic. Add the pork. Brown well on all sides. Add salt and pepper, about half a glass of white wine, and the mushrooms. Cover pan tightly, lower heat, and cook 20 minutes or until done. Serves 4.

Desserts

Gail Gibbons

  **Eve Bunting**

My mother's elderly aunt lived alone in a little town in Ireland, about ten miles from our home. Every Thursday she came by bus to spend the day. My mother always made a special dinner on Thursdays and holidays for Auntie T.

"Poor thing," she'd say. "She doesn't eat well. I like to give her something good when she comes."

So my mother would fix splendid roasts, legs of lamb, roasted chickens, salmon fresh from the river Bann. Whatever my mother made, Auntie T would eat every bite, push back her empty plate and say with satisfaction: "Good potatoes, Sissie. The potatoes are great this year."

It became a joke in our family, to be repeated after every extraordinary meal— "Great potatoes, Sissie."

After one especially remarkable Christmas dinner of turkey and all the trimmings, my mother served up a spectacular plum pudding, flaming in blue brandy. She'd been marinating the fruit for weeks. The fumes were almost enough to make the whole family inebriated. She served that pudding with such a proud flourish, and every crumb was eaten.

Afterwards Auntie T made her pronouncement. "Great potatoes, Sissie. Were they Skerry Blues?"

"And what did you think of the pudding?" my mother asked.

Auntie T pursed her lips. "I think there was a tad too much vanilla," she said.

BOOKS BY EVE BUNTING INCLUDE:

The Wednesday Surprise
Nasty Stinky Sneakers
Smoky Night
My Backpack
I Am the Mummy Heb-Nefert

Sissie's Plum Pudding

Soak:

¾ cup seedless raisins
¾ cup sultana raisins
¾ cup currants

in

½ cup stout until the kitchen smells like the local pub.

Don't nibble.

Then sometime before Christmas . . . the theory is that plum pudding gets better as it gets older (but then, don't we all?).

Mix:

½ cup flour	½ teaspoon salt
1½ cups breadcrumbs	¼ teaspoon ginger
1 cup brown sugar	½ nutmeg, grated
¼ cup finely chopped suet	½ teaspoon mixed spices

Add to the drunken fruit:

½ cup candied fruit peel	Grated rind and juice of 1 lemon
1 cup chopped almonds	3 eggs
1 apple, peeled and grated	A few dribbles more of stout

Pour over the dry ingredients. Use more stout if it's too dry. The more the merrier. Pour into greased 6-inch bowls, cover with waxed paper then with floured pudding cloths. Secure well. Boil in huge pot of water that comes ¾ up bowls, 5 to 6 hours. Serve with brandy sauce. Then lie down.

M_y *father was what they used to call a meat-and-potatoes man. He liked hearty meals, always with applesauce, and always followed by dessert (I was shocked the first time I visited a house where applesauce was the dessert). I especially loved my mother's bread pudding, and it never occurred to me why we had it so often. I grew up during the Great Depression, but even after my father lost his job, we always had plenty of eggs because he raised chickens in our backyard. And we always had leftover bread, because no one threw food away. It was good practice for the years to come when sugar, meat, coffee, and other things were rationed during World War II. My five children loved bread pudding, too, and I still make it now and then on a snowy Buffalo night.*

BOOKS BY MARGERY FACKLAM INCLUDE:

And Then There Was One: The Mysteries of Extinction
The Biggest Bug Book

Perfect Bread Pudding

2 ¼ cups of milk
  2 slightly beaten eggs
  2 cups 1-inch cubes of day-old bread
  ½ cup brown sugar

½ teaspoon cinnamon
  1 teaspoon vanilla
  ¼ teaspoon salt
  ½ cup raisins (or more)

Combine milk and eggs, and pour the mixture over the bread cubes. Stir in remaining ingredients, and pour into an 8-inch round baking dish. Place dish in a shallow pan on oven rack, and pour about an inch of hot water into shallow pan. Bake at 350° F about 45 minutes or until a knife inserted into the pudding comes out clean. It's really great served warm with a dollop of whipped cream, but it's just fine served cold.

Suse MacDonald

T*his bride's pudding is a family recipe which came to me from my mother when I got married. She copied all her favorite recipes for me.*

BOOKS BY SUSE MACDONALD INCLUDE:

Alphabetics
Space Spinners

Bride's Pudding

1 cup coconut	1 teaspoon vanilla
2 envelopes unflavored gelatin	¾ cup sugar
½ cup cold water	6 egg whites
⅓ cup boiling water	¼ teaspoon salt
1 pint heavy cream, whipped	

Butter a springform pan. Sprinkle with coconut. Soften gelatin in cold water. Pour in boiling water. Stir till dissolved. Cool (don't cool too much). Beat whipped cream till peaks. Beat in vanilla and sugar. Beat egg whites till peaks. Add salt. Beat in gelatin slowly. Fold in whipped cream and vanilla. Pour into pan. Sprinkle with coconut. Refrigerate at least 4 hours. Serve with raspberry sauce.

 A s a child, banana pudding was my favorite dessert. Growing up in the South meant that I never had to travel far to get a heaping serving at someone's home. I asked my Grandma Ruby if I could make the recipe by myself. She willingly agreed. I checked to make sure I had all of the right equipment, carefully measured out ingredients, sliced, and stirred. Sure, I cheated in a few areas. Nibbled on a few too many wafers, added extra vanilla just because I loved the taste. Then came the meringue topping. It seemed no matter how hard or fast I beat those egg whites they still looked like, well, egg whites, not the fluffy-as-a-cloud topping I'd pictured. I finally abandoned the meringue and put the pudding in the fridge to cool. When we helped ourselves to the cool dessert pudding later, Grandma Ruby and I agreed it was the best banana pudding either of us had ever tasted—with or without topping.

BOOKS ILLUSTRATED BY JAMES RANSOME INCLUDE:

Do Like Kyla
My Best Shoes

Grandma Ruby's Banana Pudding

¾ cup granulated sugar	2 cups milk
⅓ cup all-purpose flour	½ teaspoon vanilla extract
dash of salt	35 to 45 vanilla wafers
4 eggs, separated at room temperature	5 to 6 medium-sized ripe bananas, sliced

Combine ½ cup sugar, flour, and salt in top of double boiler. Stir in 4 egg yolks and milk; blend well. Cook, uncovered, over boiling water, stirring constantly until thickened. Reduce heat and cook, stirring occasionally, for 5 minutes. Remove from heat; add vanilla. Spread small amount on bottom of 1½-quart casserole; cover with layer of Nilla Wafers. Top with layer of sliced bananas. Pour about ⅓ of custard over bananas. Continue to layer wafers, bananas, and custard to make 3 layers of each, ending with custard. Beat egg whites until stiff but not dry; gradually add remaining ¼ cup sugar and beat until stiff peaks form. Spoon on top of pudding, spreading to cover entire surface and sealing well to edges. Bake at 425° F for 5 minutes or until delicately browned. Cool slightly or chill. Meringue topping optional.

Carmen T. Bernier-Grand

When I was growing up in Puerto Rico, my brother, my sister, and I couldn't stay away from my mother's delicious flans. One day, my mother put a flan in the refrigerator and warned us, "Don't you dare touch it." The next day she found the flan still in the refrigerator, but with three holes in it. "Who did this?" she asked. We shook our heads and shrugged, because we really didn't know who did it. My Tia Marta, who lived with us and was only two years older than my brother, said, "This is a job for a detective. I'll solve this mystery." She made each of us put our fingers in the holes. Whoever had a finger that fit was suspect. We each had a finger or two that fit. So, for years we accused each other of putting the holes in the flan. It wasn't until recently that it occurred to me that maybe it was Tia Marta who put the fingers in the flan. I called her. She didn't admit it, but she laughed and laughed.

BOOKS BY CARMEN T. BERNIER-GRAND INCLUDE:

Juan Bobo: Four Folktales from Puerto Rico
Poet and Politician of Puerto Rico: Don Luis Munoz Marin
Who Helped Ox?

Light, fruity, and satisfying, this dessert was a family favorite in my childhood and remains a favorite of family and guests, many of whom ask for the recipe. Despite its simplicity, a number of friends have managed to go wrong, because, I suspect, they first followed the instructions on the Jell-O package and then followed the recipe. So be warned: Never mind the package. Just do what the recipe says.

Perhaps the highest accolade I can give the dish is to say that it was liked even by my father, a man who professed to like only two kinds of food, rare prime beef and anything chocolate. He also had a list of foods that he refused to eat, headed by onions. They were not even to be cooked with the Sunday roast, lest they pollute it. But what is life without onions? Of course, they were cooked with the roast—but served separately. When onions reappeared in the hash signaling the end of the roast, my father would poke at them suspiciously and want to know what those white things were. "Celery," my mother always said firmly. "Oh," he would say and eat them up.

But Pink Pudding, with nary a trace of chocolate or prime beef, brought a smile to his face, and he never, ever had to be told that those things in the Jell-O were really celery.

BOOKS BY PATRICIA LAUBER INCLUDE:

Flood: Wrestling with the Mississippi
Hurricanes: Earth's Mightiest Storms
You're Aboard Spaceship Earth
How Dinosaurs Came to Be
Volcano: The Eruption and Healing of Mount St. Helens

Pink Pudding

1 package orange gelatin
1 cup boiling water
1 20-ounce can crushed pineapple

½ cup cold water
½ pint (or less) whipping cream

In a heatproof bowl, dissolve gelatin in boiling water. Add pineapple, with its juice, and cold water. Let cool. Gently stir in the whipped cream and chill in refrigerator.

The truth is I can think of more childhood unfavorites than favorites. My mother disliked cooking, partly because my father was an Englishman with English tastes (beef and potatoes). If Mom tried to whip up something fancy, Dad politely told her she "didn't need to go to all that trouble again," my sister sneaked hers to the dog, my brother demanded a hamburger, and I choked it down, complaining at every mouthful, no doubt. To please Dad, we lived on shepherd's pie (his favorite), fatty stew, and what my first husband dubbed bloody beef—Dad liked his rump roast rare and called the red stuff on the platter juice. My husband called it blood.

I did, however, relish one dessert, an airy concoction known as Floating Island. When Mother set it on the table, my sister, brother, and I leaned forward eagerly, inhaling its delicate aroma and admiring the pale yellow custard sea, studded with floating mounds of fluffy white meringue. It was Mom's one fancy culinary concoction, prepared only on special occasions. Even my father, who claimed to have lost his sweet tooth long ago, enjoyed Floating Island.

I haven't eaten Floating Island for years now (high cholesterol keeps me from indulging). I must also confess I've never tried making it myself. One look at the directions daunted me. Cooking is not one of my strong points, either.

BOOKS BY MARY DOWNING HAHN INCLUDE:

The Dead Man in Indian Creek
Look for Me by Moonlight
The Sara Summer

Floating Island*

Also known as Oeufs à la Neige *or* Eggs in Snow

MERINGUE:

Whip until stiff: 3 egg whites

Beat in gradually: ¼ cup sugar   2 cups milk

Whip egg whites and sugar, beating in each egg white gradually. Scald milk. Drop the meringue mixture from a tablespoon in rounds onto the milk. Poach gently, without letting the milk boil, for about 4 minutes, turning them once. Lift them out carefully with a skimmer onto a towel.

Use the milk to make custard.

CUSTARD: 3 or 4 egg yolks   ⅛ teaspoon salt

               ¼ cup sugar   2 cups milk

Beat egg yolks slightly. Add sugar and salt. Scald milk and stir slowly in a double boiler.

Place custard mixture over—not in—hot water. Stir constantly until it begins to thicken. Cool. Add 1 teaspoon vanilla, rum, or dry sherry.

Cool custard. Place meringue on top. Chill before serving. Serves 4.

---

* *The Joy of Cooking* by Irma S. Rombauer and Marion Rombauer Becker, Bobbs Merrill Company, Inc. 1973.

# Ann Turner

I have no recipes that have been passed down by my mother, as she died when I was a young adult. The only dish that I have strong memories of is her Floating Island. It was fluffy and white and melted in your mouth, and you could sort of push the meringue around as if it were an unwieldy sailboat. So it was a combination of delicious melting on the tongue along with a plaything. My parents were pretty tolerant of playing with one's food.

BOOKS BY ANN TURNER INCLUDE:

Valley Year
Grass Songs
A Moon for Seasons

The reason that some of these ingredients are not exact is that this recipe comes from my mother, who often doesn't follow a written recipe. She pours ingredients in and judges by looks, smell, and taste. My mother loves to cook and while growing up, my brothers, my father, and I were the lucky recipients. So were numerous members of our extended family. We would all get together at holiday times and eat, sing, and tell stories. My brother Bert put together a collection of some of these family recipes and stories and called it *Dancing Matzo Ball Soup*.

BOOKS BY BARBARA DIAMOND GOLDIN INCLUDE:

The Girl Who Lived with the Bears
Coyote and the Fire Stick
While the Candles Burn: Eight Stories for Hanukkah
The Passover Journey: A Seder Companion
Just Enough Is Plenty: A Hanukkah Tale

Sweet Noodle Kugel

$\frac{3}{4}$ to 1 pound of medium noodles
$\frac{1}{2}$ pint sour cream or yogurt
$\frac{1}{2}$ to 1 cup milk
$\frac{1}{2}$ to 1 pound cottage cheese
4 eggs
$\frac{1}{2}$ cup sugar
salt and pepper to taste
$\frac{1}{2}$ stick margarine or butter
1 jar cherry or blueberry pie filling

Cook noodles then drain. Add all ingredients except fruit and butter. Melt margarine or butter in a baking pan and pour in ingredients. Top with pie filling. Bake at 350° F for 45 to 60 minutes.

Cheese Latkes

1 pound of cottage cheese
3 eggs
2 tablespoons flour
1 teaspoon sugar
salt and pepper to taste

Mix together ingredients. Drop batter by the tablespoon into frying pan, using margarine to fry. Brown on each side. Serve with sour cream, jam, or syrup. A variation on the Hanukkah favorite—potato latkes.

I *grew up on my Grandma Kepniss's so delicious noodle kugel. We never had a family gathering (except Pesach, noodles aren't kosher for Passover) that didn't include my gram's amazing kugel. To tell the truth, my grams made many, many, many wonderful things to eat. But, in today's hurry-up-and-get-there world, my personal favorite of all her Jewish-Rumanian delicacies, her specialty, boiled in chicken soup and then fried in chicken fat kreplach (Jewish won ton stuffed with flanken), took so long to make (not-to-mention that they were little heart attacks in the making) that they became a lost art when Grams passed on.*

But not her kugel! Fast and easy (a secret that was kept from me until my mom decided it was time for me to take over the bring-the-kugel tradition), Grams's kugel is a 1-2-3 delicious delight. All my young life it was . . . "Invite Grandma Kepniss, she can bring her fabulous noodle kugel!" When I was an adult, this became, "Invite Grandma Sylvia, she can bring her fabulous noodle kugel!" Hopefully, now, the secret knowledge of Grandma Kepniss and Grandma Sylvia's to-die-for noodle kugel will guarantee my invitations to all future family gatherings, so I will bring my fabulous noodle kugel!

I dedicate this recipe to my grams, Anna Kepniss, and my mom, Sylvia Gordon, for all the love and sweetness they've brought into my life.

BOOKS BY STEPHANIE GORDON TESSLER INCLUDE:

Two Badd Babies
What Would Mama Do?
Upstairs
A Pile of Pigs

Grandma Kepniss's To-Die-For Noodle Kugel

As passed down to Grandma Sylvia, passed down to Stephanie Gordon Tessler

1 stick margarine
8 ounce noodles raw/flat,
   medium to large size,
   Dutch style
3 eggs
2 cups milk
3 tablespoons vanilla
⅓ cup sugar

¼ teaspoon salt
1 can crushed pineapple—small size
1 8-ounce carton small curd cottage
   cheese
⅓ to ½ cup white raisins
   a bisel crumbled corn flakes
1 glass baking dish— not too big,
   not too small

Preheat oven to 350° F. Melt margarine in dish. Mix everything (except corn flakes) in a real big bowl. Pour into baking dish (right into melted margarine). Sprinkle on corn flakes. A bisel cinnamon is optional. Bake 60 to 90 minutes or until kugel is golden brown, but not too brown (the deeper the dish—the longer you bake it). Put it all together early and store in fridge for a softer kugel. Double recipe for extra to bake and freeze or for a big family gathering or so you'll have leftovers to give away—a bisel to take home for later is a Jewish tradition almost as important as having a fabulous noodle kugel!

Fress!

M*y sons had never had much interest in cooking until they real-ized that a few hours in the kitchen could lead to extra credit in school and endear them to their teachers. They cooked their way through Spanish with tortilla casseroles and raised a letter grade on a report on New Orleans with a batch of homemade pralines. I came to realize that a request for a recipe often signaled a sagging average. Last year dur-ing exams my oldest came into the kitchen and sheepishly asked for my baklava recipe. "For Mr. Ioannides?" I asked, recalling that his geometry teacher's name was Greek. He nodded. I don't know if it helped his grade, but it was delicious. I submit this recipe for other needy students.*

BOOKS BY BETSY DUFFEY INCLUDE:

A Boy in the Doghouse
How to Be Cool in the Third Grade

Extra-Credit Baklava

FILLING:

1 cup very finely chopped walnuts   2 tablespoons sugar
1 teaspoon cinnamon

SYRUP:

¾ cup water   ½ cup honey
24 sheets of phyllo pastry, thawed

Melt one cup of butter or margarine. Brush each sheet of pastry with butter as you layer half of them in a baking pan. Spread with filling and continue layering buttered pastry. Score the top few sheets in a dia-mond pattern. Bake at 350° F for 45 minutes or until golden brown. Remove from oven and pour syrup mixture over the hot baklava. Cut all the way through and serve to your children's teachers when cool.

This recipe for apple krisp is from my Grandmother Johnson. She was born in Sweden and came to the United States in 1939. I remember as a child she would make these whenever we had extra apples in the house. Over the years I have used sugar, honey, and since we have been in Vermont, I use maple syrup. It is wonderful for a snack or a dessert, and it is healthy.

BOOKS BY GAIL GIBBONS INCLUDE:

Caves and Caverns

Frogs

Pirates: Robbers of the High Sea

 Apple Krisp

8 to 10 medium cooking apples	1/4 cup walnuts
juice of 1 lemon	1/4 cup sunflower seeds
1/2 cup butter	1 teaspoon cinnamon
1/3 cup honey	1/2 teaspoon allspice
2 cups raw oats	1/2 teaspoon salt
3/4 cup flour	1/2 cup orange juice

Peel (if necessary), pare, and slice apples. Drizzle them with fresh lemon juice. Spread half of them into a large, oblong pan.

Melt the butter and honey together. Combine with oats, flour, nuts, seeds, spices and salt. Spread half of this mixture (actually crumble, it won't really spread) onto apples in pan. Cover with the remaining apples and the rest of the topping. Pour orange juice over the top. Bake 40-45 minutes, uncovered, at 375° F. Cover if it crisps too quickly. Serves 6 to 8.

NOTES:

1. If you'd be uncomfortable leaving out raisins, you are allowed to add some. Put them in with the apples so they won't burn.
2. Throw in some cranberries for a jeweled effect.
3. Substitute pears or peaches for the apples. Reduce baking time to 25 minutes for peaches.

My mother used greening apples (from the tree where the chickens learned to fly). The apples, small and irregular in size, were too tart to eat except when cooked. Mother adapted the recipe to whatever she had on hand. I hope you do, too. This is a delicious dessert.

BOOKS BY SYLVIA HOSSACK INCLUDE:

The Flying Chicken of Paradise Lane
Green Mango Magic

Apple Brown Betty
An old recipe, possibly of New England origin

3 cups soft bread crumbs
½ cup butter, melted
¾ cup packed brown sugar
1 teaspoon ground cinnamon
about 4 large cooking apples

juice of small lemon
grated lemon peel
a few tablespoons apple juice
a favorite topping

Stir together bread crumbs and melted butter. Combine brown sugar and cinnamon. Add to buttered bread crumbs. Mix lightly and set aside. Peel, core, and slice apples. Add lemon juice and lemon peel. Layer one-third of the crumb mixture on the bottom of a casserole dish. Arrange apple slices on top. Cover with another third of the crumb mixture. Add more apple slices. Sprinkle remaining crumb mixture on top. Drizzle with apple juice. Bake about 60 minutes at 350° F. Serve warm with your favorite topping. Serves 6.

W*hen I was growing up we had rhubarb plants in our yard. I remember my mother letting me have a stalk now and then to dip in sugar and eat raw. It makes my mouth pucker now, but I thought it was a great treat back then. My mother worked full time. She didn't have time to make pies and things for a family of nine, so she always turned our rhubarb into sauce. My mother-in-law, who also grows her own rhubarb, passed this recipe on to me. Big kids (I guess they're called adults) and little kids love it. The whole pan disappears in one sitting at my house!*

BOOKS BY VIVIAN SATHRE INCLUDE:

Leroy Potts Meets the McCrooks
On Grandpa's Farm
Three Kind Mice
Mouse Chase
Slender Ella and Her Fairy Hogfather

Rhubarb Crunch

5 cups diced rhubarb
1 cup oatmeal
¾ cup white sugar
½ cup brown sugar

½ cup butter, softened, not melted
⅔ cup flour
half-and-half

Place rhubarb in greased 9 x 13-inch baking pan. Mix other ingredients (except half-and-half) until crumbly, and crumble over rhubarb. Bake in oven until rhubarb is tender—40 to 45 minutes at 325° F. Cool. Serve each piece topped with a splash of half-and-half.

\text{Jacqueline Briggs Martin}

When I was a child, rhubarb season came in early summer, following spring with its digging in the earth for dandelion greens, which we cleaned, boiled with salt pork and ate as a delicacy. Some of us called them a delicacy. To some—including my two sisters—they were bitter and tough.

But we all agreed on rhubarb. Each year my brothers and sisters and I would pull stalks of rhubarb out of the patch and try to eat them raw. But raw rhubarb is mostly sour. It is overwhelmingly sour. And each year, after a couple of bites, we decided we would wait for the cooked variety. Rhubarb has always been best in pies and cobblers. And my mother's rhubarb pie was the best of all. Even now I could eat it for breakfast, lunch, or dinner—and do when I get the chance.

When I moved away from home I went through several springs with no rhubarb. One year, when my husband and I were exploring the yard of our recently purchased house with our young children, Sarah and Justin, I found a patch of rhubarb and knew we had really found a home. We used the rhubarb for occasional pies, but Justin and Sarah preferred rhubarb cobbler. We made this recipe often in the spring, because they could help prepare it—and it tastes great with milk or topped with ice cream. Some spring nights we made a double batch and ate only rhubarb cobbler for supper.

BOOKS BY JACQUELINE BRIGGS MARTIN INCLUDE:

Good Times on Grandfather Mountain

Washing the Willow Tree Loon

Grandmother Bryant's Pocket

The Green Truck Garden Giveaway

Rhubarb Cobbler

In a pot, mix ¾ cup sugar and 2 tablespoons cornstarch. Stir in 4 cups rhubarb, sliced or cut into pieces about 1 inch long, and 1 tablespoon water. Slowly bring to a boil; cook and stir one minute. Pour into an 8-inch round or 9-inch square baking dish. Sprinkle with a few shakes of cinnamon. For biscuit topping, see below. Bake in oven at 400° F for 20 minutes.

BISCUIT TOPPING FOR COBBLER:

Sift together 1 cup sifted all-purpose flour, 1 tablespoon sugar, 1½ teaspoons baking powder. With a pastry blender, cut in ¼ cup butter or margarine until it is the size of coarse crumbs. Mix together ¼ cup milk and 1 slightly beaten egg; add to dry ingredients, stirring just to moisten. Drop by spoonfuls on the hot fruit.

APPLE COBBLER:

If you cannot find rhubarb you can make apple cobbler. Combine 1 cup sugar, 1 tablespoon cornstarch, ½ teaspoon cinnamon, ¼ teaspoon nutmeg. Toss with about 6 cups of cut-up tart apples. No need to peel the apples. Cook and stir over medium heat until almost tender, about 5 to 7 minutes. Pour into 8-inch round or 9-inch square baking dish. Top with the biscuit mixture and bake at 400° F for 20 minutes.

When I was 13, I joined a teen-age square-dance group. My whole family square danced. As a tradition, every October my mother calls for a church group's Halloween party at a towering Victorian mansion. This historic mansion rises tall by the Sacramento Delta River. I have enjoyed going along to help Mom teach square-dance steps to the new dancers. After we dance in a barn surrounded by pear orchards, everyone is invited into the gorgeous mansion for pie and ice cream. One special pie dessert is so delicious that my mother asked for the recipe and now makes it for special occasions, such as my own almost-Halloween birthday. And now that I have children of my own, we all come to the Delta mansion as a family and my kids square-dance, too.

BOOKS BY LINDA JOY SINGLETON INCLUDE:

Opposites Attract
Love to Spare
Teacher Trouble

Luscious Layered Dessert

LAYER 1:

  1 cup melted margarine   1 cup flour   1 cup chopped nuts

  Mix margarine, flour, and nuts. Pour into 9 x 13-inch pan. Bake 350° F for 20 minutes. Let cool

LAYER 2:

  1 cup powdered sugar   4 ounces creamed cheese

  1 cup nondairy whipped topping

  Mix powdered sugar, creamed cheese, and whipped topping. Spread over cooled layer 1 mixture.

LAYER 3:

  4-ounce instant chocolate pudding   2 ½ cups milk

  4-ounce instant vanilla pudding   1 teaspoon vanilla

  Beat pudding, milk, and vanilla mixture until thick and creamy. Spread over layer 2.

LAYER 4:

  Spread remaining whipped topping over top of layer 3. Top with grated chocolate bar or nuts. Chill overnight.

*O*h, *those cool Colorado summer nights. My brother, sister, and I would bolt from the dinner table before dessert to get outside—playing keep away, hide-and-seek, or kick the can until it was too dark to see. At dusk, the air would be filled with mothers calling their children inside. So, in we'd go to enjoy a bowl of homemade strawberry shortcake, along with the requisite battle over who would get to lick the whipped cream off the beaters.*

BOOKS BY DIAN CURTIS REGAN INCLUDE:

The *Ghost Twins* series
Dear Dr. Sillybear
Princess Nevermore
The Monster of the Month Club Quartet

Mrs. Curtis's Summer Strawberry Shortcake

STRAWBERRIES:

In a large bowl, slice fresh strawberries, sprinkle with sugar to taste, and beat to bring out the juice. Refrigerate.

DESSERT BISCUITS:

1¾ cups all-purpose flour
2½ teaspoons baking powder
1 teaspoon salt
1 tablespoon sugar
⅛ cup butter
¾ cup milk

Stir ingredients with fork for 30 seconds. Knead dough on a floured board for another 30 seconds. (The secret to a flaky biscuit is a light, quick stirring and kneading.) Pat dough to ½-inch thickness. Cut with biscuit cutter dipped in flour. Bake 10 to 12 minutes at 450° F.

OLD-FASHIONED WHIPPED CREAM:

Chill bowl, beaters, and carton of cream in refrigerator for at least two hours. Beat cream with mixer on medium speed until cream begins to thicken. Lower speed and sprinkle in sugar to taste. Beat till cream peaks.

THE GRAND FINALE:

Break biscuits into pieces in dessert bowls. Spoon strawberries and juice over the top. Finish off with a dollop (or two or three) of whipped cream.

My mother regarded cooking as an unnecessary evil. Rheumatic fever in her childhood left her without a sense of smell or taste, which was helpful when changing diapers for five kids, but did nothing for the subtleties of food preparation. Her own personal diet consisted of Velveeta cheese with Ritz crackers and Pepsi spiked with Port wine; supper for the rest of us was usually hot dogs and burnt french fries, or meat loaf made from ground beef and oatmeal. Period. I know we had salt in the cabinet—we used it to melt ice on the front steps, but if we had anything like garlic or basil, it never found its way into the meat loaf.

Sometimes she made something delicious, like peaches on toast. It appeared whenever the market had a run on overripe peaches, which were free. I've made it with whole grain bread and Pam instead of margarine, but the original is still better.

BOOKS BY DIANE DE GROAT INCLUDE:
Trick or Treat, Smell My Feet
Roses Are Pink, Your Feet Really Stink

Peaches on Toast

Wonder bread	fresh peaches (very ripe)
margarine	sugar

1. Peel and cut peaches into large chunks, removing pits and any brown spots. Place in a bowl and sprinkle with sugar. Let sit until the sugar is dissolved and syrupy.
2. Spread margarine onto both sides of bread. Fry until browned and greasy.
3. Spoon some peaches over the hot bread, and eat it with a knife and fork. Yum.

Cookies and Cakes

Illustration © 1997 by Marla Frazee from *The Seven Silly Eaters*,
reprinted by permission of Harcourt Brace & Company.

I'm a homey kind of person. Is anything more homey than a kitchen with cookies in the oven? It was one of my favorite things as a kid to help my mom or grandma drop teaspoonfuls of oatmeal cookie dough onto the trays to bake. A bit of finger licking was required, of course, and the wonderful sweet-spicy smell that came from the oven as they baked was another treat. As a mom, cookie baking was one of my favorite things, too, and I always loved eating them just as much as my kids did. When my youngest showed signs of being allergic to some of the additives in commercial foods, I went a little crazy on keeping everything natural and healthy. Some of it, homemade mayonnaise and yogurt and fresh baked bread, was really good. But my kids resisted my attempts to add tofu dishes to our menus, and totally refused the brewers yeast in the peanut butter. They still talk about the time "Mom went on her health-food binge." This oatmeal cookie recipe is one we all agreed was a keeper, though. It's good and healthy, but still quite tasty.

BOOKS BY ANNA GROSSNICKLE HINES INCLUDE:

Daddy Makes the Best Spaghetti
Big Like Me
When the Goblins Came Knocking
Miss Emma's Wild Garden
When We Married Gary

Good-and-Healthy Oatmeal Cookies

$3/4$ cup margarine or butter
$1/4$ to $1/2$ cup brown sugar*
3 tablespoons to $1/4$ cup sugar*
2 eggs
2 teaspoons vanilla
$1/4$ cup water
1 cup flour
1 teaspoon salt

$1/2$ teaspoon baking soda
1 teaspoon cinnamon
2 cups oatmeal
1 cup bran
1 cup wheat germ
1 cup chopped walnuts
1 cup raisins

Cream margarine and sugars. Beat in eggs, vanilla and water. Add flour, salt, soda, and cinnamon, then mix in other ingredients. Drop onto greased cookie sheets. Bake at 350° F for 12 to 15 minutes.

*I started with the larger amounts of sugar then cut down to the smaller amounts.

In my childhood home, Granny did most of the cooking, because Mama was what was then a rare breed—a working mother. Although it was the 1950s, Granny was still cooking for the Depression, and it was a good thing, too, since it was difficult to make ends meet in our three-generation household.

But at Christmas time, Mama always took over the kitchen for the holiday cookie baking. The cookies were simple, plain sugar dough, but when Mama had rolled it out thin and cut it into shapes with our motley collection of cutters, we children were set to making them spectacular with candy decors. We sprinkled on colored sugar and silver shot and nonpariels. My favorite was cinnamon hots, which I deployed liberally. My brother and sister tired quickly, but I loved making the plain shapes come alive with color. And, most of all, I loved cooking with Mama!

I baked Mama's cookies with my own children when they were growing up. I bake them still with my young friends, or with my grown children and their children, visiting for the holidays. For me, Christmas wouldn't be complete without Mama's Christmas Cookies.

BOOKS BY ELLEN HOWARD INCLUDE:

Circle of Giving
Her Own Song
The Log Cabin Quilt
A Different Kind of Courage

Mama's Christmas Cookies

3½ cups flour	1½ cups sugar
1 teaspoon baking powder	3 eggs, well beaten
½ teaspoon salt	1½ teaspoons vanilla
1 cup shortening	

Sift flour; measure; add baking powder and salt; sift again. Cream shortening; add sugar gradually and continue to beat until light. Add well-beaten eggs and blend thoroughly; add vanilla. Combine dry ingredients and creamed mixture; mix thoroughly and chill. Roll as thin as possible on a lightly floured board and cut with cookie cutters. Decorate with candies. Bake at 400° F for 6 to 10 minutes. Makes about 6 dozen thin cookies.

BOOKS BY LESLIE TRYON INCLUDE:

Albert's Alphabet
Albert's Field Trip
One Gaping Wide-Mouthed Hopping Frog

The Deco-Duck-in's Toll-House Cooky

Preheat oven to 350° F.

½ pound (2 sticks) softened butter
1 cup light brown sugar, packed
¾ cup granulated sugar
1 teaspoon vanilla extract
one whole egg plus one egg yolk
1 tablespoon instant espresso granules
dissolved in 1 tablespoon warm water

3 cups all-purpose flour
1 teaspoon salt
1 teaspoon baking soda
½ teaspoon cinnamon
2 cups chocolate chips
1 cup chopped nuts

Cream butter and two sugars together until light and fluffy. Beat in vanilla, eggs, and dissolved instant espresso mixture. Continue to beat mixture for at least 2 more minutes. Add dry ingredients. Mix until flour is well combined. Mixture will be sticky. Add chocolate chips and chopped nuts.

Roll walnut-sized balls of batter in palms of hands. Place on waxed paper-lined cookie sheet and press with fingers to flatten slightly.

Bake at 350° F for 8 to 10 minutes. Remove from oven and allow cookies to cool on sheet. Remove to a cooling rack. Yields 60 cookies.

Albert's grandmother's favorite variation on this cookie (and a real time saver):

Grease a baking dish and spread cookie dough evenly. Bake for 8 to 10 minutes. Cut into squares and serve with a scoop of vanilla ice cream.

My brother, sister, and I loved helping Mom make Christmas cookies. I'm not sure if it's because she let us eat bits of raw dough (which I thought was better than cooked dough) or if it was because the decorating turned into a friendly competition. Mom rolled out the dough, then we chose the shapes to cut, although if we got too carried away with one shape, she'd stick another cookie cutter in our hands. When the cookies were cooled, it was time to decorate! Sometimes we'd start with white frosting and add sprinkles on top. Other times we'd be clever and use maple frosting for the reindeer because it had a brown tint, then add a cherry for its nose. When we felt especially creative, we'd spread maple on white frosting cookies to create hair on angels or hats on snowmen. I enjoyed painting my candy canes with red stripes or decorating my Christmas trees with nut garland and silver dragée ornaments. We had to be fast, too, because there was a window of creativity before the frosting hardened and the sprinkles didn't stick. But the best past of making these cookies was eating them.

BOOKS BY NATASHA LAZUTIN WING INCLUDE:

Hippity Hop, Frog on Top
Jalapeño Bagels

Christmas Cookies

4 cups flour	1½ cups sugar
2½ teaspoons baking powder	2 teaspoons vanilla
½ teaspoon salt	2 eggs plus milk to make ⅔ cup
⅔ cup vegetable oil	

<small>FROSTING:</small>

4½ cups powdered sugar	2 teaspoons vanilla
½ cup softened margarine or butter	about 3 tablespoons milk

Sift flour, baking powder and salt in large bowl. Add oil and blend with fork. Beat sugar, vanilla, egg and milk mixture together until a light color. Stir into flour. Chill 1 hour. Roll on floured cutting board. Cut out shapes with Christmas cookie cutters. Bake at 400° F for 7 minutes or until edges turn a light golden brown. Cool and decorate with frosting, sprinkles, nuts and maraschino cherries.

For the frosting, divide it into smaller bowls and add a few drops of food coloring (one drop at a time until you get the color intensity you want) to make red, green or yellow frosting. Or if you want to flavor the frosting, cut the vanilla back to 1 teaspoon and add 1 teaspoon of maple, almond, or mint flavoring. (You may want to cut back the vanilla altogether and have a stronger flavoring by adding more of the other flavor.) My mother never seemed to measure when it came to the frosting, so she was always adding more flavoring, or she'd accidentally put too much coloring in so she'd have to add more powdered sugar and milk. Sometimes she'd add maraschino cherry juice for both color and flavor. Like my mother, you may want to experiment with the frosting to make it to your liking.

BOOKS BY MARGERY CUYLER INCLUDE:

Barry, Bear, and the Bad Guys
That's Good! That's Bad!
From Here to There

Squirrel Bars

½ cup peanut butter
½ cup butter
¾ cup brown sugar
2 eggs, beaten

2 teaspoons vanilla
1 cup flour
1 teaspoon baking powder
6 ounces chocolate chips

Mix together first 3 ingredients. Add eggs and vanilla. Stir in flour and baking powder. Spread mixture in a greased 9 x 13-inch pan. Sprinkle chips on top. Bake 3 minutes at 350° F. Take out and marbelize by swirling knife through batter. Return to oven for another 18 to 20 minutes. Cool and cut into bars to serve. Serves 8 to 10.

I *grew up in San Diego, California, where the weather is mild much of the year. Family picnics to the back country often included my grandmother. She loved to bake goodies for me and my two brothers. On our picnics we looked forward to her deviled eggs and sandwiches filled with cream cheese, chopped black olives, and walnuts—on white bread without the crusts. My brothers and I especially loved her graham cracker cookies. She always put them in a rectangular-shaped tin, with waxed paper spread between each layer of cookies. I inherited my grandmother's recipe book and remember her every time I make these cookies.*

BOOKS BY GINGER WADSWORTH INCLUDE:

Laura Ingalls Wilder: Storyteller of the Prairie
Desert Discoveries
Tomorrow is Daddy's Birthday
John Muir: Wilderness Protector

Gramma's Graham Cracker Cookies

2 cups plus 2 tablespoons graham cracker crumbs, or 15 graham
     crackers, rolled out fine
1 6-ounce package semisweet chocolate chips
1 14-ounce can sweetened condensed milk
½ can chopped walnuts

Preheat oven to 325° F.

Mix together all the ingredients. Batter will be stiff. Grease 10½ x 6-inch pan with margarine, then flour lightly. Pour mixture into pan and spread evenly with knife. Bake about 30 minutes in the oven. Don't overbake or they will dry out. Cut while still warm and roll in powdered sugar.

I go to writer-group meetings, not so much to have my writing criticized, but to eat the treats. My fellow writers and artists really know how to lay out a bountiful spread of cookies and cakes, dips and drinks, and even full dishes like crepes and salads. My mouth is watering even as I write.

One day, I went to a meeting at which the hostess, an artist, served some delicious chocolate cookies studded with almonds. They were different because they were chocolaty, nutty, and yet they were not too sweet.

I couldn't stop eating them. The hostess had to move the plate away from my end of the table. I wasn't letting anyone else have any. After I kept reaching across the table, she said, "Maybe I should save some for the baby."

"Baby?!" I asked. "Your baby doesn't even eat chocolate cookies!" After the hostess ushered me to the door, I vowed I would find a way to enjoy those cookies again. So I studied many cookbooks and tried many recipes. After finding a recipe I liked, and after adding a little bit of this and taking away a little bit of that to the mixture, I came up with these Chocolate Almond Cookies. (This recipe can also be found in my book, The Children's Book of Kwanzaa.) Try this really easy recipe for yourself, and you'll find out, as I did, that you'll have to move the plate away from all those little hands that keep reaching for the yummy chocolate cookies. That is, if you want any cookies to yourself. Good eating!

BOOKS BY DOLORES JOHNSON INCLUDE:

Now Let Me Fly: The Story of a Slave Family
Papa's Stories
Your Dad Was Just Like You

Chocolate Almond Cookies

1 cup sugar

2 eggs

⅓ cup unsweetened cocoa powder

1½ cups flour

1 teaspoon baking soda

½ cup slivered blanched almonds

½ teaspoon vegetable oil

Preheat oven to 350° F. Beat sugar and eggs with a spoon in a medium-sized mixing bowl until well mixed. In another bowl, combine cocoa, flour, baking soda, and almonds. Add this to the sugar and egg mixture. Drop spoonfuls of batter onto a baking sheet greased with the vegetable oil. Bake for 15 to 20 minutes. Let cookies cool on the baking sheet for 2 minutes and then remove to a wire rack to cool completely. Makes 3 dozen cookies.

My mother, Anna Cross Giblin, taught high-school French in Cleveland, Ohio, before she married my father, who was a lawyer. After their marriage, she enrolled in law school and graduated with honors three years later. A year after that, I was born, interrupting her career plans. At that point, Mother became what in the 1930s was called a housewife.

She didn't give up her own interests, though. If it came to a choice between cooking Sunday dinner and reading a book, she would opt for the book and we would go out for dinner to a country inn or a restaurant in Cleveland. In spite of this, Mother was an excellent cook when she wanted to be.

She was a firm believer in balanced meals, and introduced me to all the wonderful possibilities of vegetables, cooked plainly so the natural flavors came through. I still remember the squashes she served—acorn, butternut, and summer—not to mention the eggplants, green beans, zucchini, broccoli, parsnips, peas, and spinach. I learned to like all of them when I was a boy, even spinach—and I still do.

But Mother's culinary gifts shone brightest in the treats she made for the holidays: chocolate brownies that were crisp on the outside and chewy within; sugar cookies with little colored sprinkles on top; and especially her oatmeal cookies. Like everything she baked, they were sweet but not too sweet, moist but not too moist, and they contained just the right number of dark raisins.

I couldn't resist sampling the cookies between meals, even though Mother was sure to say, "Jim, you'll spoil your lunch!" (or dinner, as the case might be). Secretly, though, I think she was pleased that I liked them so much. After I'd grown up and left home, she always baked a batch of those oatmeal cookies when I returned for a visit.

BOOKS BY JAMES CROSS GIBLIN INCLUDE:

Writing Books for Young People
From Hand to Mouth
Be Seated: A Book About Chairs
The Dwarf, The Giant, and the Unicorn: A Tale of King Arthur

Anna Cross Giblin's Oatmeal Cookies

1½ cups shortening
1½ cups sugar
1 egg
1 cup flour
1 cup rolled oats

½ teaspoon cinnamon, cloves, and
   baking soda
½ cup raisins, plumped in boiling water
2½ tablespoons raisin juice

Cream shortening and sugar. Add egg. Stir in flour, oats, spices, and soda. Add raisins and juice. Shape into 1-inch balls. Drop on baking pan. Bake at 350° F for 10 to 12 minutes.

In our little town of Plymouth, Michigan, we were blessed with Terry's Bakery. Every birthday was celebrated with one of Terry's magnificent cakes. The ritual never varied. So it was no surprise when I wrote Laura Charlotte that I gave Laura the exact same birthday cake—"a tall chocolate cake with butter cream frosting and pink sugar roses on top." Besides cakes and homemade breads, Terry's made donuts—trays and trays of them, all fresh that morning. The glazed ones were my favorite, so big and so soft that the tip of your nose got sticky when you took that first bite. However, donuts were just for special Saturday mornings and cakes just for birthdays. Then I discovered their molasses cookies. Crunchy, with sprinkled sugar, soft and chewy underneath, they were the perfect anytime treat. Later, long after Terry's Bakery had disappeared, a friend gave me her recipe for soft molasses cookies. I was thrilled. Of course, these cookies aren't quite as soft or as chewy or as perfect (no cookie could be), but still they are delicious, if you've never had one of Terry's, I think you'll like these very much indeed.

BOOKS BY KATHRYN O. GALBRAITH INCLUDE:

Laura Charlotte

Holding Onto Sunday

Roommates

Roommates and Rachel

Roommates Again

Soft Molasses Sugar Cookies

¾ cup shortening
1 cup sugar
¼ cup molasses
1 egg
2 teaspoons baking soda

2 cups sifted all-purpose flour
½ teaspoon cloves
½ teaspoon ginger
1 teaspoon cinnamon
½ teaspoon salt

Melt shortening in a 3- or 4-quart saucepan over low heat. Remove from heat; allow to cool. Add sugar, molasses, and egg. Beat well. Sift together soda, flour, cloves, ginger, cinnamon and salt. Add to first mixture. Mix well and chill. Form in 1-inch balls, roll in granulated sugar and place on greased cookie sheet, 2 inches apart. Bake in hot 375° F oven for 8 to 10 minutes (about 1 minute after the top begins to crack). Makes 4 to 5 dozen.

M_y *Grandmother Mayes had a tremendous effect on my life. She is the only person I've ever known who could read, watch TV, smoke, carry on an intelligent conversation, drink Tab, keep an eye on dinner in the oven, and do complicated needlework all at the same time—and do each of them well. Through her I was introduced to a world of music and literature that formed the basis of my career as a storyteller, as well as a lifetime of good eatin'!*

BOOK BY WALTER MAYES AND VALERIE LEWIS:

Walter and Valerie's Best Books for Kids: A Lively and Highly Opinionated Guide

Walter the Giant Storyteller's Grandma's Brown Sugar Brownies

4 eggs
1 pound brown sugar (light, preferred)
¼ cup butter
1½ cups sifted flour
1½ teaspoons baking powder

1 teaspoon salt
½ teaspoon maple flavoring
½ teaspoon vanilla
1 cup walnuts
confectioners' sugar

Preheat oven to 350° F. Spray a 9 x 13-inch cake pan with nonstick cooking spray.

In a double boiler, warm eggs, brown sugar, and butter. Watch closely. Stir constantly until ingredients are thoroughly mixed and lightly bubbling. Cool slightly, then stir or blend in flour, baking powder, salt, flavorings, and walnuts.

Pour batter into pan, cook 25 minutes. Do not over cook. These are best when they are still moist and chewy.

Cut into squares when cool. Next day, sprinkle with confectioners' sugar.

When I came home every day from school, my mother would be waiting for me with a glass of milk and a plate of cookies. We would sit at the kitchen table and talk. I loved this small locket of time with my mother. When I went away to college, I missed my family. My mother started sending me cookies with a kiss to let me know everyone sent me their love. This cookie has become a family favorite and I wove part of its story into my book, The Lemon Drop Jar.

BOOKS BY CHRISTINE WIDMAN INCLUDE:

The Star Grazers
Housekeeper of the Wind
The Lemon Drop Jar
The Willow Umbrella
The Hummingbird Garden

Peanut Blossoms

½ cup butter
½ cup peanut butter
½ cup sugar
½ cup brown sugar
1 egg
2 tablespoons milk

1 teaspoon vanilla
1⅓ cups flour
1 teaspoon baking soda
½ teaspoon salt
one bag of Hershey's Kisses

Cream together butter and peanut butter. Gradually add sugars. Cream well. Stir in egg, milk, and vanilla. Add dry ingredients and mix well.

Shape dough into balls the size of Ping-Pong balls. Roll in granulated sugar. Bake on ungreased cookie sheet at 375° F for 8 to 10 minutes, until slight cracks begin to form on top of cookies. Take out of oven and place an unwrapped Hershey Kiss on top of each cookie. Return to oven for 1 minute. Take out of oven and cool on rack. Makes 3 to 4 dozen.

Our house on Pershing Avenue was where all the kids in the neighborhood came to play, and of course they were always ready for a treat. St. Louis summers can be miserably hot—too hot to bake, for sure. One day, I found this quick, no-bake recipe on the back of a graham cracker box. I could make dozens of bite-sized munchies in minutes, and all without lighting the oven. Wow! Imagine making cookies in a cool kitchen. But would the kids like them? After the first few bites, the nibblers announced that the cookies were "kool," thus the name: Summer Cool, Kool Cookies, Chill.

BOOKS BY PATRICIA McKISSACK INCLUDE:

Black Diamond: The Story of the Negro Baseball Leagues
Sojourner Truth: Ain't I a Woman?
Christmas in the Big House, Christmas in the Quarters

Summer Cool Cookies

16 graham crackers, crushed
1 medium-sized bag of small
   marshmallows
1 cup chopped pecans

1 cup sugar
½ stick of margarine
½ cup evaporated milk
1 teaspoon vanilla

Put graham crackers, marshmallows, and pecans in a large bowl. Mix sugar, margarine and milk in a saucepan. Bring mixture to a slow boil, stirring constantly. When the mixture begins to boil, lower heat to medium and cook for 5 more minutes. Remove from heat and stir in vanilla. Pour hot mixture over dry ingredients in the bowl. Mix well. Drop portions of the mixture onto waxed paper. Let cool for about an hour before serving. Yummy! Makes about 3 dozen.

Marion Dane Bauer

This is a family recipe, one which came from my mother's mother. When Mother was growing up, these cookies were called "Orson's cookies," after the one boy in the family who especially loved them. My brother and I always called them "Grandma's cookies," and I used to snitch raw dough to eat (which Mother said wasn't good for my stomach) when we rolled them out.

This is the recipe I use for the bear-shaped gingerbread cookies in my picture book, Jason's Bears. *The recipe appears at the end of the story so that young readers, with some help, can make their own bear-shaped cookies and, in eating them, conquer their own bears.*

BOOKS BY MARION DANE BAUER INCLUDE:

On My Honor
Am I Blue: Coming Out from the Silence
Jason's Bears

Jason's Ginger Bear Cookies

$\frac{1}{2}$ cup hot water
1 teaspoon baking soda
1 cup sugar
1 cup shortening
1 teaspoon ginger
$1\frac{1}{2}$ teaspoons cinnamon

$\frac{1}{2}$ teaspoon ground cloves
$\frac{1}{2}$ teaspoon nutmeg
1 teaspoon salt
1 cup dark molasses
2 eggs
$5\frac{1}{2}$ cups flour

Stir baking soda and all the spices into the hot water. Set spice mixture aside and mix sugar and shortening together until they are smooth. Then, stir the spice mixture, molasses, eggs, and flour into sugar and shortening mixture. If necessary, add up to a half cup more flour to make a stiff dough for rolling. Cover dough and chill in the refrigerator for at least 1 hour. Once the dough is chilled, roll it on a floured surface, cut out shapes, and bake on a greased or nonstick pan at 350° F for 10 or 12 minutes.

When I was growing up, there were no package mixes for cakes and brownies. I have tried a few since then, but I don't like mixes. I like to see all the ingredients and know what they are. I also think home-made tastes better.

My only problem with these chocolate brownies is that they are so good that I could eat a whole batch. They are very fattening. The solution, I have found, is to invite my family and friends to help me eat them so I don't eat too many myself.

BOOKS BY JEAN MARZOLLO INCLUDE:

The *I Spy* series

In 1492

In 1776

Snow Angel

Ten Cats Have Hats

Easy, Delicious Chocolate Brownies

This recipe for easy, delicious chocolate brownies was given to me by my mother. What's great about these brownies is that you only need one pan to make them. You don't need a bowl. You melt butter and chocolate in the pan, and then you use the pan as a bowl. The only trick is to use a thick pan so the butter and chocolate do not burn.

⅓ cup butter	2 unbeaten eggs
2 squares unsweetened baking chocolate	1 teaspoon vanilla
1 cup sugar	½ cup flour

Melt butter and chocolate in a large, heavy saucepan over low heat. Remove from heat and add sugar, eggs, and vanilla. Stir, then add flour. Mix well. Bake in greased 8 x 8-inch pan at 325° F for 30 to 35 minutes. They are done when you stick a toothpick in and it comes out clean. Don't let them burn.

I *liked most things that were not leafy green and healthy. I was very fond of sweet things, probably because sweets weren't often on the menu at our house. Of all the desserts that appeared from time to time, coconut cake, and lemon meringue pie were my favorites. I like the cake because it was sweet, moist, creamy, crunchy, and messy.*

I like the pie because of its different tastes and textures. It was fun to slice off perfectly clean pieces with the meringue and lemon still together. The end crust came last but not least.

BOOKS BY ELLEN STOLL WALSH INCLUDE:

Brunus and the New Bear
Hop Jump

Coconut Cake

Preheat oven 375° F. Grease and flour 2 8-inch round cake pans.

2 cups sifted yellow cake flour	$\frac{1}{2}$ cup shortening
$1\frac{1}{4}$ cups sugar	$\frac{3}{4}$ cup milk
$1\frac{1}{2}$ teaspoons baking powder	$1\frac{1}{4}$ teaspoons vanilla
$\frac{3}{4}$ teaspoon salt	2 eggs, unbeaten

Sift together dry ingredients. Add shortening, milk, and vanilla. Mix well, scraping sides and bottom often. Add eggs. Beat 30 seconds longer. Divide batter evenly between pans. Bake 25 to 30 minutes, or until tester comes out clean. Cool.

ICING:

$\frac{1}{3}$ cup soft butter or margarine	milk or cream
3 cups sifted confectioners' sugar	$\frac{1}{2}$ cup flaked coconut
$1\frac{1}{2}$ teaspoons vanilla	

Cream butter with sugar using electric mixer. Add vanilla. Mix. Add milk or cream 1 tablespoon at a time until the icing is a desired spreading consistency. Frost the cake, immediately patting the finished product all over with flaked coconut.

My mom made the best chocolate cakes in the world. At least, that's how I remember it. And she didn't just bake for special occasions—sometimes she made a cake just for fun. But no matter what recipe my sisters and I try from the cookbook our mother usually used, it never tastes quite the same to me. That's why I'm always on the lookout for a recipe that somehow matches my memories. This recipe for Buttermilk Chocolate Cake, which I received from a wonderful lady named Mary Ho, has become one of my favorites for birthdays and special occasions. But sometimes, usually on a stormy winter weekend, I'll bake it for my kids just for fun.

BOOKS BY DEBORAH HOPKINSON INCLUDE:
Sweet Clara and the Freedom Quilt
Birdie's Lighthouse

Buttermilk Chocolate Cake

2 cups flour
2 cups sugar
1 teaspoon baking soda
1 cube margarine
½ cup cooking oil

1 cup water
4 tablespoons cocoa
2 slightly beaten eggs
½ cup buttermilk
1 teaspoon vanilla

Sift together flour, sugar, and soda. Set aside. In a large saucepan combine margarine, oil, water, and cocoa. Bring to a rapid boil. Remove from heat and add sifted dry ingredients, mixing well with wire whisk. Add eggs, buttermilk, and vanilla. Mix to blend thoroughly and pour into a lightly greased 9 x 13-inch baking pan. Bake at 400° F for 20 to 25 minutes.

FROSTING:

1 cube margarine

4 tablespoons cocoa

6 tablespoons buttermilk

1 pound box powdered sugar
($\frac{1}{3}$ at a time, mixing well)

1 teaspoon vanilla

1 cup chopped nuts (optional)
vanilla (if desired).

In medium saucepan combine margarine, cocoa, and buttermilk. Bring to a boil. Add powdered sugar ($\frac{1}{3}$ at a time, mixing well).

Spread warm frosting over hot cake. (You may turn slightly cooled cake out on a tray and frost top and sides, or leave in pan and poke into cake evenly with fork so frosting will seep into cake from top.)

Like all children, I looked forward to my birthday for weeks. Getting gifts was exciting, and the birthday party was fun, but a special highlight every year was being able to choose what cake Mother would make for me. Not that I got creative—I always selected the same deep, dark chocolate cake with pure white icing. I loved the color contrast as well as the combination of moist, soft cake and slightly grainy frosting. And besides, what child, given a choice, would choose anything but chocolate?

BOOKS BY DOROTHY HINSHAW PATENT INCLUDE:

Flashy Fantastic Rain Forest Frogs
Return of the Wolf
West by Covered Wagon
Biodiversity
Quetzal: Sacred Bird of the Cloud Forest

Devil's Food Cake with Seven-Minute Icing

CAKE:

1¾ cups sifted cake flour
1 teaspoon salt
1 teaspoon soda
½ cup cocoa
1½ cups sugar

2 eggs, unbeaten
1 teaspoon vanilla
⅔ cup milk
½ cup shortening

Sift dry ingredients. Add sugar, eggs, vanilla, milk, and shortening. Mix well. Divide batter between two greased 9-inch cake pans. Bake at 375° F for 20 to 25 minutes, or until toothpick comes out clean.

SEVEN-MINUTE ICING:

2 unbeaten egg whites
1½ cups sugar
5 tablespoons cold water

½ teaspoon cream of tartar
1 teaspoon vanilla

Place ingredients in top of double boiler and beat until blended. Place pan over rapidly boiling water. Beat constantly with electric mixer or wire whisk for 7 minutes. Remove from heat. Add vanilla. Continue beating until desired consistency.

As a child I lived in a neighborhood that had no kids my age to play with. So, when the Truitts moved in next door and I saw those five kids, I made friends with them in a hurry. This cake was a tradition in their house for every birthday and special event. It wasn't long before it became my requested birthday cake, too. Tradition has it that you stir a penny, a nickel, a dime, and a quarter into the batter for an extra surprise when you cut the cake.

BOOKS BY SUSAN TAYLOR BROWN INCLUDE:

Can I Pray with My Eyes Open?
When Jasper Closed His Eyes

American Beauty Cake

1 2-ounce bottle of red food coloring	1 cup buttermilk
3 tablespoons milk chocolate cocoa (instant)	2½ cups sifted flour
	½ teaspoon salt
½ cup shortening	1 teaspoon vanilla
½ cup sugar	1 tablespoon vinegar
2 eggs	1 tablespoon baking soda

Mix food coloring with cocoa. Let stand. Cream shortening and sugar. Add eggs, buttermilk, flour, salt, and vanilla. Beat well and remove from mixer. Add vinegar and baking soda. Mix by hand. Pour into two greased and floured 8-inch pans. Bake at 350° F for 30 to 35 minutes. Cut each layer in half lengthwise to make four layers. (Use a piece of thread to cut them.)

ICING FOR AMERICAN BEAUTY CAKE

4 tablespoons flour	½ cup shortening
1 cup milk	1 cup sugar
pinch of salt	2 teaspoons vanilla
½ cup butter or margarine	

Mix flour, milk, and salt in a jar and shake until completely smooth. Pour into small saucepan and cook until it thickens to consistency of heavy cream; cool completely. Mix well butter, shortening, sugar, and vanilla. Add cooked flour mixture and beat in mixer till very fluffy. (Make half of this recipe for an ordinary 2-layer cake.)

A t age seventeen, I flew from my home in Wisconsin to California to attend college. I couldn't afford to go back for vacations or my birthday, so Mom would send me her cake.

It arrived at my dorm in perfect condition, not a crumb out of place. The secret? She placed the cake in a plastic bag and packed it in popcorn. Not styrofoam popcorn, but edible movie-theater popcorn!

When one of my famous packages arrived, word spread fast. Party time! My friends and I had two delicious desserts—the fabulous chocolate cake and the popcorn.

The cake represents my childhood to me. Mom made the cake for my birthdays, for parties at my elementary school, and for my good report cards. When I married in 1982, this recipe was my wedding cake. Everyone thought I was crazy. Back then, everyone had boring white cakes decorated with beautiful but tasteless white frosting. A chocolate wedding cake with chocolate frosting? It just wasn't done. But I did it.

To this day, when I make Mom's cake, I smell a faint scent of popcorn.

BOOKS BY ELIZABETH KOEHLER-PENTACOFF INCLUDE:

Curtain Calls
Explorers
Louise the One and Only
Wish Magic
Help! My Life Is Going to the Dogs!

Mom's Chocolate Cake

¾ cup butter or margarine
2¼ cups sugar
1½ teaspoons vanilla
3 eggs
3 1-ounce squares unsweetened
    chocolate, melted

3 cups sifted flour
1½ teaspoons baking soda
¾ teaspoon salt
1½ cups ice water

Cream butter, sugar, and vanilla with mixer. Add eggs, beating until light and fluffy. Blend in melted chocolate. Sift together dry ingredients. Add alternately with water to chocolate mixture. Pour batter into three 8-inch-layer greased pans. Bake at 350° F for 30 to 35 minutes. Cool. Put layers together and frost with fudge frosting. (For cupcakes, bake 25 minutes. Makes about 40 cupcakes.)

MOM'S FUDGE FROSTING

3 squares unsweetened chocolate
3 cups sifted powdered sugar
⅔ cup brown sugar, packed
1 teaspoon vanilla
¼ cup margarine
½ cup heavy cream or canned evaporated milk

Combine everything but powdered sugar and vanilla. Bring to boil until chocolate and butter are melted. Then add powdered sugar and vanilla.

I remember I loved to serve this cake to my friends when they came over for lunch or to play. Then, after they'd raved about how great the cake was, I'd tell them it had mayonnaise in it. They'd make terrible faces and not believe me, but they still had seconds on the cake!

BOOKS BY PEGGY KING ANDERSON INCLUDE:

The Fall of the Red Star
Safe at Home
Coming Home

Mayonnaise Cake

2 cups flour
4 tablespoons cocoa
2 teaspoons baking soda
1 cup sugar

1 cup mayonnaise
1 cup water
2 teaspoons vanilla

Mix all. Bake at 350° F till tests done, about 1 hour.

What I remember is that we had to bake it until it cracked in the middle and then it was done, otherwise it came out soggy. Delicious when frosted with cocoa-powdered sugar frosting. (Dump a pound box of powdered sugar in a bowl with a big glop of unsweetened cocoa powder, and a sprinkle of salt. Stir, add a half stick of softened margarine or butter, pour on a few spoonfuls of hot coffee or milk to melt, and stir, adding coffee or warm milk to desired consistency.) Amounts of cocoa can vary according to taste.

When my mother and I visited my maternal grandmother, we always took a stroll around the grounds to see what her green thumb had produced. After the tour my grandmother always served us a treat. Sometimes she had a fresh batch of No-Fuss Cupcakes. The aroma of these cupcakes brings back memories of the grandmother we called Booger—clay pots on the windowseat that held the promise of summer flowers, glass jars turned upside down to shelter rose cuttings, and an old bayonet she kept in her garden to dig up seedlings to send home with us. Most of all, I remember the rosebud corsages she made for Mom and me to wear on Mother's Day each year. By tradition a red rose was worn in honor of a living mother and a white rose for one who had passed on. One year Booger didn't have enough red roses for two corsages so she used pink for Mom's. I still remember the twinkle in her eye when she said pink was appropriate because she was ailing.

BOOKS BY DEANNE DURRETT INCLUDE:

Code Talkers, Library of American Indian History Series
Healers, American Indian Lives Series
The Importance of Norman Rockwell
Angels
The Importance of Jim Henson

No-Fuss Cupcakes

Preheat oven to 350° F. Place paper baking cups in muffin tin.

1/3 cup shortening	1/2 teaspoon ginger
3/4 cup sugar	1/2 teaspoon cinnamon
1 well-beaten egg	1/2 cup milk
1/2 teaspoon salt	1/2 cup chopped dates
2 teaspoons baking powder	1/2 cup chopped nuts

Cream shortening and sugar. Add egg. In separate bowl, sift together dry ingredients. Add milk to creamed sugar mixture alternately with dry ingredients. Mix after each addition. Fold in dates and nuts. Fill cups 1/2 full of batter. Bake until done (when toothpick comes out clean, about 20 minutes.)

I *have always loved chocolate. Chocolate cake was the only cake I ever wanted for my birthday. I must have been asked if I'd like something different for a change. But only chocolate cake would do. So every year that's what Mother made. I have no idea what recipe she used. This is one I have adopted. It came from a church cookbook from a small town in southern New Hampshire. I got it from a friend many years ago, and it's so good I've never tried another recipe for chocolate cake.*

Mount Monadnock stands alone in southern New Hampshire between Keene and Peterborough. The peak, 3,165 feet high, is easily accessible by several foot trails of varying degrees of length and difficulty.

On clear days the views from various points on the mountain are quite amazing. You can see the snow-covered White Mountains to the north over 150 miles away . . . the skyline of Boston 85 miles to the southeast and the campus of the University of Massachusetts at Amherst 56 miles to the southwest.

On a busy Sunday afternoon the top of the mountain looks like a rookery, but it's covered with people, not birds. The best time to visit is during the midweek before or after peak summer holidays.

It's worth the hike to the top. Then go home and have some chocolate cake.

BOOKS BY MARGOT APPLE INCLUDE:

Blanket

*Ready . . . Set . . . Read and Laugh: A Funny Treasury
for Beginning Readers*

Mount Monadnock Chocolate Cake

½ cup butter (softened)

1½ cups sugar

2 eggs (beaten)

2 squares chocolate, unsweetened
    type (melted over double boiler)

1¾ cups all-purpose flour

1½ teaspoons cream of tartar

½ cup milk

1 teaspoon baking soda

¾ cup boiling water

1. Cream together butter and sugar. Add eggs. Mix. Add chocolate. Mix well.
2. Sift flour with cream of tartar.
3. Add flour to chocolate mixture alternately with milk; first flour, then milk, etc.; end with flour. Mix thoroughly.
4. Dissolve baking soda in boiling water (it will fizz). Quickly add to batter. Stir in and "beat like hell" till bubbles appear. This helps cake puff up and be light.
5. Pour into two 9-inch greased cake pans. (I line pan bottoms with waxed paper greased on both sides.)
6. Bake at 325° F for 45 minutes.

Cool 15 or 20 minutes. Remove from pans. Place on rack. Cool till cold before frosting.

CLASSIC FUDGE FROSTING:

4 squares unsweetened chocolate	dash of salt
2 tablespoons butter or margarine (melted)	½ cup milk
4 cups confectioners' sugar (unsifted)	1 teaspoon vanilla

Combine sugar, salt, milk, and vanilla. Mix. Add melted chocolate and margarine to sugar/milk mixture. Blend well. Let stand till it thickens to spreadable consistency. Spread quickly! Add small bit of milk if it gets too thick.

margot apple

Thelma was our neighbor, Mrs. Seeton. She had six kids. She made this cake every day of the year. Six kids. One cake per day. To a boy with only one brother, these were baffling, amazing statistics. When my mother made Thelma's chocolate cake, it lasted almost a week. When I grew up I got married and had a family of my own. One day my wife baked a cake, part of which we ate for dessert. Later that night, craving a snack, I went for the cake. It was gone. Vanished. I stood in the kitchen, both hungry and enlightened, for now it was I who had six kids—and a perfect understanding of why Thelma Seeton baked a cake every day.

BOOKS BY JERRY SPINELLI INCLUDE:

Space Station Seventh Grade
Who Put That Hair in My Toothbrush?
Maniac Magee
The Library Card
Wringer

Thelma's Chocolate Cake

2 cups flour
2 cups sugar
2 teaspoons baking soda
4 squares chocolate
½ pound butter

1 cup water
2 eggs
1 cup sour milk
1 teaspoon vanilla

Mix flour, sugar, and soda. Heat chocolate, butter, and water on stove—enough to melt chocolate and butter. Add to dry ingredients. Beat together eggs, milk, and vanilla. Add to mixture and mix. Bake in tube pan at 350° F for about 1 hour.

When I was a young girl, Mary Jo Myers lived next door and was my dear friend. Her mother made this cake. I persuaded Mrs. Myers to give the recipe to my mother, who often baked it to the delight of my sister, my brother, and me. I brought the recipe with me when I married. My three children have made it the official birthday cake at our house. I guess you can't go wrong when you pair the two great childhood favorites—chocolate and peanut butter.

BOOKS BY PATRICIA HARRISON EASTON INCLUDE:

Stable Girl
Summer's Chance

Iris's Chocolate Cake with Chocolate-Peanut Butter Icing

Preheat oven to 350° F.

⅓ cup cocoa	1 teaspoon vanilla
1 cup boiling water	2½ cups flour
½ cup butter, room temperature	2 teaspoons baking soda
2 cups sugar	½ teaspoon cream of tartar
2 eggs	pinch of salt
1 cup cold water	

Mix cocoa and boiling water. Cool. Cream butter (room temperature) and sugar. Add eggs and cold water. Mix well. Stir in cocoa mixture and vanilla. Sift together dry ingredients and add to cocoa mixture. Stir to mix. Pour batter into a greased and floured 8 x 12-inch pan. Bake at 350° F for about 45 minutes, until it pulls slightly away from the sides of the pan. Cool and ice with Chocolate-Peanut Butter Icing:

In an electric mixer, beat:

¼ cup butter, room temperature	enough milk to bring to
¼ cup peanut butter, room temperature	spreading consistency
¼ cup cocoa	(add milk one tablespoon
1-pound box of confectioners' sugar	at a time)

The family birthday dinner. After clearing the main course, my sisters Kate and Nancy run around the house, dousing lights. I stay at the table, wiggling in my seat. I am the birthday girl. "It's ready, it's ready," my brother Tim calls.

"Everybody sit down before the candles go out!" my dad adds. The kitchen door swings wide and we ooh and ah as my mother walks in with the cake, candles blazing. My oldest sister, Susan, starts the song: Happy birthday to you . . .

And another chocolate sponge cake becomes the centerpiece of another birthday celebration. Mom had many creative ways to decorate the outside: with a dolly in the middle, it became an elaborate gown; or with animal crackers circling, a small carousel, but always the inside was the same. These days my husband bakes the chocolate sponge cake on my birthdays, and he decorates it by sculpting peaks and swirls in the luscious white icing.

I have a photo of my great-grandmother, Jessie Brownlie Pennycook, who began this birthday tradition over a hundred years ago. She had a waspish thin waist and a tight-mouthed look. I like to think that, like us, she relaxed on her birthday and allowed herself second and even third helpings.

BOOKS BY LAURA MCGEE KVASNOSKY INCLUDE:

Two, Three, Play with Me!
Pink, Red, Blue, What Are You?

Chocolate Sponge Cake

7 eggs, separated, plus 1 yolk
1½ cups sugar
1 teaspoon vanilla
¾ cup ground chocolate

¾ cup boiling water
1⅛ cups flour
2 teaspoons baking powder
dash salt

Separate eggs. Beat yolks until thick. Add sugar gradually and continue beating. Add vanilla. Dissolve chocolate in water and add to mix-

ture. Sift dry ingredients and fold into batter. Beat egg whites with salt until stiff and fold in.

Bake at 325° F for 60 to 70 minutes in a springform pan with open center core (angel food cake pan will work, too). Invert the cake on a cake stand or narrow-necked bottle as it cools.

FLUFFY WHITE FROSTING:

1 cup sugar
⅓ cup water
⅓ teaspoon cream of tartar

2 egg whites (⅓ cup)
1½ teaspoons vanilla

Slowly bring to a boil in small saucepan: sugar, water, and cream of tartar. Boil to soft-ball stage: syrup forms a soft ball when dropped into iced water. While syrup is boiling, beat egg whites (⅓ cup) until stiff enough to hold a point. Pour hot syrup very slowly in a thin stream into the stiffly beaten egg whites, beating constantly on high. Add vanilla. Beat until frosting holds its shape.

M*y mother was a good cook. Solid, wholesome food was her sig-nature, mainly Eastern European and even more so, Russian. The one frivolous item of which she was inordinately proud was her Daffodil Cake. It would sit nobly on a tall silver-and-glass cake plate, bringing us a bit of spring during those long dark New England winters.*

Into a sponge cake pan she would pour the two batters alternately, so that when the confection was sliced, each of us had a perfumed white-and-gold delight—a daffodil. As a child, it intrigued me! Sadly, I never asked her for the recipe when I married.

BOOKS BY SHULAMITH OPPENHEIM INCLUDE:

I Love You, Bunny Rabbit
The Hundredth Name
What Is the Full Moon Full Of?

Daffodil Cake

Preheat oven to 350° F. Use angel cake tube pan. Do not grease! All ingredients should be at room temperature.

1½ cups sifted flour (resifted twice more)
1¼ cups sugar
10 egg whites
    Rind of 1 orange, grated

6 beaten egg yolks
1 teaspoon vanilla
½ teaspoon salt
1 teaspoon cream of tartar

Sift flour three times. In a separate bowl whip egg whites until frothy. Add salt and cream of tartar. Whip at high speed until whites hold a peak. Fold in sifted sugar gradually. Separate batter into two equal parts in separate bowls. Into one half of the batter fold ¾ cup of the sifted flour, grated orange rind, and beaten egg yolks, adding a lit-tle at a time.

Fold into the other half, a little at a time, the remaining sifted flour plus vanilla. Layer batters in ungreased tube pan, alternating colors. Bake approximately 45 minutes or until done. Cool upside down on neck of bottle.

Pies

Nicole Rubel

# **Marla Frazee**

Fudge Pie

2 squares Bakers chocolate or
   3 tablespoons cocoa
1 stick butter or margarine
1 cup sugar
$\frac{1}{4}$ cup flour

2 eggs, unbeaten
2 teaspoons vanilla
4 pinches of salt
$\frac{1}{2}$ cup chopped nuts

Melt Bakers chocolate or cocoa and butter in saucepan. Then add remaining ingredients.

Fudge pie is best when it's already past your bedtime. Your parents are exhausted and staring at the TV. You sneak into the kitchen and begin melting the butter and chocolate in a saucepan.

Your parents call out, "What are you doing in there?"

Say, "Nothing!" Stir until melted.

Add the sugar, flour, eggs, vanilla, salt, and nuts to the same pan.

Quickly pour this goop into an 8-inch pie pan, and put it on the top rack of the oven for 25 minutes at 350° F.

Your parents call out, "Hey, what's all the racket?"

Now you can answer with, "I made fudge pie!"

Of course, they won't send you to bed now. They'll make room for you on the couch. You snuggle in next to them, but not for long, because fudge pie tastes best when it's slightly moist, like a brownie.

Get it out of the oven.

Eat it topped with ice cream, or just plain, along with a glass of milk.

Don't worry about the dishes.

Your parents will do them after you go to bed.

My grandmother was a young German widow who came to America with two children to meet a man she only knew through letters. They met in New York for five days and decided they got along well enough to marry. They lived on a small Idaho wheat farm that had a wood stove and a pump at the kitchen sink.

When I was a child, my father often requested lemon pie for his birthday. As my mother baked, I would look at the worn recipe and wonder about wood stoves, and the words "take from the fire" and "brown in a low oven." It didn't sound like anything we did on our electric stove, and Grammie was no longer around to ask.

Later, when I grew up, I wrote in my spare time and worked as a cook. I learned to read between the lines of Grammie's recipe; a low oven is 250 to 300° F, and a custard should always be stirred as it thickens. But the directions below are purely Grammie's. No time for fuss or extra words, just the bare minimum to make a fabulous, light-as-a-feather, lemon pie.

BOOKS BY PATRICIA WITTMANN INCLUDE:

Go Ask Giorgio

Scrabble Creek

Buffalo Thunder

Grammie's Lemon Pie

1 prebaked pie shell, using your favorite recipe

½ cup superfine sugar

1 tablespoon flour

14 eggs, separate yolks from whites

1 large lemon, grate peel and juice

1 tablespoon water

½ teaspoon salt

½ teaspoon baking powder

Pour sugar into pan—add flour and mix. Add egg yolks, lemon rind and juice, water, and salt. Cook in double boiler until thick.

Beat egg whites with baking powder until stiff. Fold in ½ cup sugar.

Take custard from fire and add butter. Fold ½ of egg white mixture into custard while still warm. Pour into pie shell and top with the rest of the egg whites. Brown in low oven.

When I visited my Grandmother Long in the mountains of north Georgia, it was like going back to an earlier time. Until I was grown she lived in a house with no electricity and no indoor toilet. A spring provided the family water and its refrigeration. She cooked on a wood-burning stove, and I can still remember how the first wisps of smoke smelled when they escaped in little curls around the stove lids. Her fried apple pies were made from apples she'd raised and then dried. She served them on all occasions: family dinners, church dinners-on-the-ground, food offerings to bereaved families. Of course she served them when she had birthday dinners for Great-grandpa Fields. Ma Long kept giving him dinners "in case he doesn't live until next year." He lived to be 106.

When at nearly a hundred Ma Long came to visit me and my husband on the old family farm where we live, she walked over the place, advising us on how to make the most of the land. Her final piece of wisdom was, "Plant you some apple trees out beyond the barn. Fried apple pies always come in handy."

BOOKS BY FAYE GIBBONS INCLUDE:

Some Glad Morning
King Shoes and Clown Pockets
Night in the Barn
Mountain Wedding

Ma Long's Fried Pies

PASTRY:

2½ cups all-purpose flour   ½ tablespoon shortening
1 teaspoon salt   6 tablespoons cold water (or less)

Combine flour and salt; cut in shortening until particles are like very small peas or coarse meal. Sprinkle water over mixture and stir with a fork until mixture is moist and holds together when pressed between hands in a very brief kneading motion. Form into ball and chill slightly before rolling to about ⅛-inch thickness. Cut into 5-inch circles and stack circles between waxed paper.

FILLING:

1 8-ounce package dried apples   ½ teaspoon nutmeg
½ cup sugar (or sugar to taste)   water
½ teaspoon cinnamon   cooking oil

Cook apples. Drain. Mash fruit with sugar and spices. Place about 2 tablespoons of fruit mixture on half of each pasty circle. Fold pastry in half. Moisten the edges with water and seal well with fork tines. Lightly prick top surface. Heat 1 inch of cooking oil in heavy skillet to about 375° F. Carefully place pies in hot oil, allowing room to turn them easily. Brown until golden on each side. Remove to absorbent paper. Serve warm or cold.

In our country home in western New York, my mother was some- times expected to cook venison, pheasant, rabbit, muskrat, and a vari- ety of freshwater fish in the summertime. She was not an outstanding cook, but as a child and adult I loved her pies. They included rabbit pot pie, but were mostly apple, cherry, and rhubarb.

I have come to link my mother and rhubarb pie, because the recipe is hers, and until she died in 1995, I could get all the rhubarb needed in a great rhubarb patch behind her barn. Even now, the rhubarb I take from my garden comes from plants transplanted from that spe- cial place. (By the way, you can make several pies and freeze them, then unleash that delicious spring and early summer taste of rhubarb in other seasons.)

The crust recipe is also special, as it was used long ago in Russia by my wife, Susan's, grandmother. I could go on for pages about crust- making. Sometimes a bit more water or flour must be added to have the dough roll out well. The end result can even be affected by humidity in the air. I don't get enough year-round practice at crust-making, so, while some of mine are beauties, others are ugly messes. The rhubarb part is always wonderful.

BOOKS BY LAURENCE PRINGLE INCLUDE:

One Room School
Everybody Has a Bellybutton
Dinosaurs! Strange and Wonderful
Taking Care of the Earth: Kids in Action

Mom's Rhubarb Pie

CRUST:

    5 tablespoons shortening   2 tablespoons ice water
    1 cup flour

Blend flour and shortening with a fork. Then add water and knead the dough into a lump. With a rolling pin, roll it out into a circle at least 9 inches across. Then wind the crust gently onto the rolling pin so you can easily lift and unroll the crust into a pie plate. Trim the edges, then bake in a 400° F oven for 10 minutes.

PIE:

    3 cups chopped rhubarb stems   1 tablespoon melted butter or
1½ cups sugar   margarine
    3 tablespoons flour   2 well-beaten eggs
    1 teaspoon nutmeg

Chop rhubarb. Blend sugar, flour, nutmeg, and butter. Add eggs and mix well. Fill the pie crust evenly with the chopped rhubarb, then pour the sweet fluid over the rhubarb. Bake at 450° F for 10 minutes, then at 350° F for another 30 minutes.

When I was a child, my Italian grandparents would come and stay with us for a week every summer. To me, they were very exotic. They spoke funny, they ate strange things, and my grandmother's hair was silver-long threads that reached beyond her waist. Every morning she would comb it out and then put it up into braids on top of her head. Then the cooking would begin. She made pastas, sauces, and cookies that I'm ashamed to say I would turn my nose up to, except for my grandmother's rice pie. Oh, how I loved that rice pie. I loved it so much that I even wrote a book about it called, Nana's Rice Pie. *The story tells about a young girl who misses her father, who is out rice farming. In her wisdom, the grandmother entices the granddaughter into making a rice pie. The whole time they share their heritage of family, farming and love. No, the story does not tell my story, other than the memory of a loving grandmother cooking with her granddaughter. But Grandma's sweet rice pie recipe is included.*

BOOKS BY LAURIE LAZZARO KNOWLTON INCLUDE:

Why Cowboys Need a Brand
Why Cowboys Sleep with Their Boots On

Nana's Rice Pie

| 1 cup instant rice | 1 cup water | 1 teaspoon salt |

Let water come to a boil. Add rice. Stir. Cover and remove from heat. Let sit 5 minutes.

FILLING:

3 eggs	¼ teaspoon cinnamon
1 12-ounce can evaporated milk	⅛ teaspoon nutmeg
1 teaspoon vanilla	cooked rice

Preheat the oven to 350° F. Beat eggs. Add milk, sugar, vanilla, cinnamon, and nutmeg. Mix in cooked rice. Nana's Rice Pie tastes wonderful with or without a pie shell. If you don't want the pie shell, just pour the mixture into the pie pan and bake. Bake in the oven for 45 minutes. Serve hot or cold.

PIE SHELL:

1 cup all-purpose flour

½ teaspoon salt

⅓ cup plus 1 tablespoon shortening

2 to 3 tablespoons cold water

Measure flour and salt into a bowl. Cut in shortening. Sprinkle water over the flour mixture 1 tablespoon at a time. Mix until all of the flour forms a ball and almost clears the side of the bowl. Roll the dough out on a floured surface with rolling pin, spreading it out 2 inches larger than the pie pan. Gently place the pie shell into pan.

*O*kay, so I admit that I have this . . . well, this thing for chocolate. I can't resist it, have no self-control around it, absolutely love it. As far as I'm concerned, it's one of the major food groups.

If this sounds extreme to you, kind of warped, even, then blame my mom. It's her fault. If it hadn't been for the chocolate pies she kept making when I was a kid and then forcing me to eat them, I probably would be normal today.

On the other hand, if you aspire to have a thing for chocolate, too, then follow this recipe very carefully. It just might change your life.

BOOKS BY TOM BIRDSEYE INCLUDE:

Airmail to the Moon
Soap! Soap! Soap! Don't Forget the Soap!
I'm Going To Be Famous
Just Call Me Stupid
Tarantula Shoes

Mom's Chocolate Meringue Pie

9-inch baked pie shell

FILLING:

1 cup sugar	2 ½ cups milk
5 tablespoons cornstarch	3 egg yokes, lightly beaten
4 heaping tablespoons cocoa	½ teaspoon vanilla
½ teaspoon salt	¼ teaspoon almond extract

In saucepan, combine dry ingredients and mix well. Stir in milk and mix until smooth. Cook over medium heat, stirring until thickens. Stir half of hot milk mixture into egg yokes and mix well. Pour back into saucepan, bring to boil, stirring. Remove from heat. Stir in vanilla and almond extract. Pour into pie shell.

MERINGUE:

3 egg whites at room temperature   6 tablespoons sugar
¼ teaspoon cream of tartar

In medium bowl with mixer at medium speed, beat egg whites and cream of tartar until soft peaks form. Gradually beat in sugar, 2 tablespoons at a time. Continue to beat until stiff peaks form. Spread over warm filling, sealing to the edge of the crust. Bake 7 to 10 minutes, or until golden. Cool on wire rack away from drafts, husbands, and children.

Even as June Cleaver set the tone for women of the day, my mother had little to do with household chores. Although she held great respect for women who managed households, she had chosen a different course for her life. She was a businesswoman, and one who rarely entertained the notion of cooking. Yet, three times a year my grandfather—her father—would pay us a visit, and my mother would fly into a frenzy of cooking activity. I always looked forward to those visits because Papa would entertain us with tales of his travels hither and yon. They no doubt planted the seed for my own wanderlust.

Papa's visits were always a surprise, but one given away by my mother's simple request: "Punkin, will you run out and pick me three or four nice lemons?"

To this day, a sampling of Papa's Lemon Pie brings warm memories of those long-ago visits, and produces a smile as I recollect my mother's frenzied activity in a kitchen largely unfamiliar to her. And I hear Papa's customary grace: "God, bless the cook!"

BOOKS BY LARRY DANE BRIMNER INCLUDE:

Cory Coleman, Grade 2
Max and Felix
Merry Christmas, Old Armadillo
Rolling . . . In-line!
Rock Climbing

Papa's Lemon Pie

1 cup plus 1 tablespoon sugar	1 tablespoon grated lemon rind
3½ tablespoons cornstarch	3 beaten egg yolks
1 cup milk	¼ cup butter
½ cup lemon juice	1 cup sour cream

Mix together the above ingredients, except egg yolks, butter, and sour cream. Cook over moderate heat until thick, stirring constantly. Remove from heat. Introduce 2 or 3 tablespoons—one at a time—of the hot cornstarch mixture to the beaten egg yolks. (Beat vigorously after each addition.) Then pour the yolk mixture into the cornstarch mixture. Return to moderate heat, and stirring all the while, cook until it comes to a boil. Cook an additional minute. Add butter and cool to room temperature. When cool, stir in sour cream. Pour into a 9-inch baked pie crust. Top with meringue.

MERINGUE:

3 egg whites (reserved from above)	¼ teaspoon cream of tartar
pinch of salt	½ cup sugar

Place first three ingredients in a bowl and beat on high speed with an electric mixer until the whites hold a peak. Reduce speed, and add sugar a little at a time. Spread meringue over pie filling. Bake immediately in 300° F oven until the peaks are lightly colored. Cool completely in a draft-free place. Then refrigerate. Serve chilled.

S.D. (Steve) Schindler

M_y *mom made fruit pies from scratch; by that, I mean she made the pie crust. She was undoubtedly taught by my grandmother who also made pies, but my mom's were better, thanks to Betty Crocker, circa 1930 something. Although she made them regularly, they were so good that we asked for them on our birthdays instead of a cake. My sister, Betsy, always wanted cherry; I asked for blueberry. Mom also made rhubarb, strawberry, raspberry, peach, and apple pies. When I left home, I realized I couldn't do without them, so I wrote my mom for the recipe.*

BOOKS ILLUSTRATED BY S.D. SCHINDLER INCLUDE:

Twelve Days of Christmas
Big Pumpkin
Children of Christmas: Stories for the Season

Apple Pie

CRUST:

2 cups flour
1 teaspoon salt

½ cup vegetable oil
¼ cup milk

FILLING:

6 to 7 apples, peeled, cored, and
 sliced (Granny Smith is the best)
1 cup sugar

¼ cup flour
1 tablespoon cinnamon

For crust, mix ingredients well in bowl; add vegetable oil and milk. Stir with fork. With hands, shape into a ball; then cut in half. Roll out ½ between 2 sheets of waxed paper to fit a 9-inch pie pan (crust is thin, about ⅛-inch thick). Peel off 1 sheet of waxed paper and flip crust side down onto pie pan; peel off other sheet carefully.

For filling, mix sugar, flour, and cinnamon in bowl; add apples and stir to coat the apples. Spoon onto pie crust. Roll out other half of crust; peel off one sheet of waxed paper, and flip crust side down onto filling. Peel off other sheet carefully.

Mold the edges with fingers (or tool) to seal the two crusts. Prick top crust with fork in 5 or 6 places. Place on cookie sheet in case it oozes. Bake at 350° F for 50 minutes or until top crust is browned. Cool to room temperature before cutting.

This pie is really good with whipped cream or vanilla ice cream or, if you're German like my dad, with a big wedge of sharp cheddar cheese (yuck!). Pie making takes a bit of practice, and some people never get it. To this day, my wife refuses to even try.

Rotten Ralph loves this pie, and I bake it for him when he's good!

BOOKS BY NICOLE RUBEL INCLUDE:

Conga Crocodile
The Ghost Family Meets Its Match
Cyrano the Bear

Apple Pie

pie crust (top and bottom)   dash salt
lots of Rome Beauty apples   many dashes cinnamon
almost 1 cup sugar   dash nutmeg
juice of 1 lemon

Peel, slice, and throw apples in large bowl. Add sugar, lemon, cinnamon, salt, and nutmeg. Mix together.

Pour into bottom pie crust. Place top crust over. Bake at 375° F for 1 hour.

I've been baking pies since I was no older than twelve. Until recently, my parents had several acres of pie-cherry trees on their property in Eugene, Oregon. Every summer I picked cherries, pitted them, and froze them in plastic bags for later use in pies. Occasionally a cherry pit or two turns up in a piece of pie . . . usually in a piece eaten by my husband, as luck would have it. Fortunately, he hasn't cracked a tooth yet.

BOOKS BY SUZANNE WILLIAMS INCLUDE:

My Dog Never Says Please
Library Lil
Emily at School
Mommy Doesn't Know My Name

Ma's Sweet-Tasting, Mouth-Watering Cherry Pie

FILLING:

4 to 5 cups pitted pie cherries   3 tablespoons tapioca
(fresh or frozen, thawed)   1⅓ cups sugar

Drain cherries, if juicy, reserving ½ cup of the juice to add back in. Mix cherries and juice with sugar and tapioca. Let stand for 15 minutes before pouring into pastry-lined pie pan.

PASTRY FOR 9-INCH PIE:

2 cups sifted flour   ⅔ cup shortening
1 teaspoon salt   ¼ to ⅓ cup water

Combine flour and salt in bowl. Cut in shortening with a pastry blender. Add water a little at a time, mixing until flour starts to clump. Use fingers to gather the dough, pressing it to form a ball. Divide dough in half for top and bottom crusts. Roll out bottom crust and place in pie pan. Add filling. Dot with 1 tablespoon butter (if desired). Use a fork to poke holes in the top crust before placing over top of filling. Seal edge and pinch to form a fluted edge. Bake 400° F, about 45 minutes (until crust is nicely browned and juice begins to bubble up).

Sprinkle top of pie with sugar immediately after removing from oven. Cool several hours before serving.

Tasty Treats

Richard Jesse Watson

I *was born on Trinidad, in the West Indies. Almost half of the people from Trinidad have ancestors who came from India a hundred or so years ago. Many of our favorite foods are Indian—and most of those are North Indian. This sweet is a popular one and among the simplest to make. It is often served at Hindu religious ceremonies when an overly pale Mohan Bhog is judged to be a worrisome sign of slipshod preparations. My children have American tastes and Mohan Bhog is one of the few Trinidad foods they enjoy. It was they who nicknamed this sweet "Play Dough to Eat."*

None of our traditional foods are prepared from written recipes, and Mohan Bhog is generally made by men, in really huge quantities. I had never made it myself until I came to America. It took a lot of experimenting before I could make even a small quantity and get it right. This recipe is the result of that experimenting.

BOOKS BY VASHANTI RAHAMAN INCLUDE:

Read for Me, Mama
Oh Christmas Tree

Mohan Bhog (Play Dough to Eat)

½ cup white flour
½ teaspoon baking powder
¼ teaspoon ground cardamom
⅛ cup (2 tablespoons) sugar

1 tablespoon raisins
½ cup milk
1 tablespoon butter (preferably unsalted) or clarified butter

In a dry pot with a heavy bottom and no nonstick coating (1-quart size for this quantity), parch flour over medium-high heat to a pale golden-brown color (a little paler than roasted peanuts and a little darker than raw pasta). Stir frequently for even browning and to prevent scorching. Be patient, it only seems to take forever.

Sift parched flour with baking powder and cardamom into a small bowl. Add sugar and raisins and mix with milk to a little-thicker-than-dropping consistency. It should be almost the color of peanut butter.

In the same pot, wiped clean of flour, heat butter to fragrance (do not let it begin to brown). Still over heat, stir in flour mixture until all butter is completely absorbed. Remove from heat. Do not overcook, or sweet will be too crumbly.

Serve by spooning into clean hands or dessert bowls. Eat with the fingers, using the thumb and first two fingers of the right hand to form and pinch off bite-sized lumps. Or, if preferred, gently shape into bite-sized balls before serving.

This is best eaten fresh, within hours, but it can be stored in an air-tight container overnight at room temperature, or for a few days in the refrigerator.

The recipe can be multiplied, but beyond 2 cups of flour it begins to get overly demanding of time and energy.

My three brothers and I had enormous appetites when growing up. The chant "Mom, what's there to eat?" was heard about our house day and night. To save her sanity, my mother became The Snack Queen. She prepared us delicious snacks, so that we boys could survive in between meals. Here is one of Mom's snack inventions that my brothers and I really loved.

BOOKS ILLUSTRATED BY ROBIN SPOWART INCLUDE:
Mama, If You Had a Wish
Sometimes I Feel Like a Mouse: A Book About Feelings
Inside Outside Christmas, (which he also wrote)

Dry Roasted Garbanzos

2 cups cooked garbanzo beans (can be made from scratch or from a can)
½ teaspoon garlic powder

½ teaspoon salt (add only if canned beans were salt free)

Preheat oven to 350° F. Mix all the ingredients together and spread on a lightly greased cookie sheet. Cook for 30 minutes or until the garbanzos are crisp on the outside. Makes 2 cups.

M*y grandfather would fix this for me (it was his favorite, too).*

BOOKS BY DAVID MCPHAIL INCLUDE:

Annie and Company
Something Special

Sunday-Night Supper
Crackers and Milk

3 pilot crackers broken into a bowl
2 pieces of stale bread (heels are best if you have them), torn into
    bite-sized pieces and added to the crackers

Toss lightly with fingers. Add a sprinkle of sugar, and then add milk
and/or cream.

W*hen I was a child, hearty meals with lots of meat, potatoes, vegetables, and desserts were in fashion. Since then trends have changed; lighter, leaner meals with less meat, less starch, less fat, and more vegetables and fruits are considered correct. Lifestyles have changed in other ways, too. Furniture is lighter. Clothes are less formal. Language and behavior are more casual. Through all the changes, this raisins and almonds snack has endured. It's been part of my Jewish heritage, immortalized in a song called "Raisins and Almonds," and found in Mindy, my first children's book; served as a snack among candies and lots of family photographs, when I was taken to visit relatives as a child; and now found in gourmet groceries and health food stores as raisins/nuts, or with dried fruit and seeds added, as tropical or trail mix. Whatever the name, it's delicious—always has been and still is! Some good things never change.*

BOOKS BY VICKY SHIEFMAN INCLUDE:

Mindy
Good-bye to the Trees
Sunday Potatoes, Monday Potatoes

Raisins and Almonds (A Healthy Snack)

½ bowl of raisins
½ bowl of almonds (or shelled peanuts, cashews, pecans, brazil, or
    mixed nuts)

Mix the raisins and nuts together.
Serve in a nice bowl to company, or enjoy just for yourself and your family.

When I was a little girl growing up in Clearfield, Pennsylvania, there was a woman who lived with my family, helping my mother with the cooking, household chores, and raising my brother and me. Her name was Ethel, and she was as dear to us as our grandmother. She was an excellent cook—and an imaginative one, too. I remember her pie crust trimmings cut into triangles, baked, topped with slices of sharp cheddar cheese, and baked again 'til the cheese was crisp and bubbly. Heaven!

BOOKS ILLUSTRATED BY BETSY LEWIN INCLUDE:

No Such Thing
Somebody Catch My Homework
A Thousand Cousins

The only entertaining my parents did when I was growing up in the sixties were cocktail parties. These snacks are great with drinks. I grew up in Vermont, which makes the best cheddar cheese, so we always use extra sharp. It might be too much for some!

BOOKS BY ASHLEY WOLFF INCLUDE:
Come with Me
Stella & Roy

Cheese Biscuits

½ cup butter (room temperature)
2 cups extra-sharp cheddar cheese
   (finely shredded)

1 cup flour
¼ teaspoon cayenne
   pepper powder

Cream butter and cheese together. Add flour and cayenne. Mix until it looks like corn meal. Roll into 2 rolls, each 1½ inches in diameter. Wrap and refrigerate until firm. Slice into ¼-inch rounds. Bake at 350° F for 5 to 10 minutes or until edges brown.

The Fourth of July is not complete without cherries! When I was little, we would always go to the most wonderful neighborhood Fourth of July picnic. All the neighbors brought a dish to pass. The kids ran wild, playing and eating while the parents sat back and laughed and talked the day away. In the evening we'd lay our blankets on the lawn and watch the fireworks with ooos! and aaws! But even better than the fireworks were the cherries and dip. Mmmm! I can almost taste them now!

BOOKS BY LAURIE LAZZARO KNOWLTON INCLUDE:

Why Cowboys Need a Brand
Why Cowboys Sleep with Their Boots On

Fourth of July Cherries and Dip

3 pounds of cherries, washed

CHERRY DIP:

Mix together the following:

1 pint sour cream	1 teaspoon lemon juice
¼ cup brown sugar	

TOPPINGS:

Brown coconut in the oven. Chop walnuts into small bits.

Hold cherry by the stem, dip the cherry into sour cream dip, then dip into toppings. Yum!

Papaya—*the best possible thing to eat.*

This is truly the fruit of the gods, without question. In my opinion nothing better has ever been invented. It's even better than Junior Mints and coffee ice cream. I've become more civilized with papaya since my youth, when I would with savage hunger paddle in from a day of hard surfing and grab a firm yellow papaya off somebody's tree, rip it open, and devour it on the spot—and boy, were they good that way. Ca-rumba! Now, though, in my—ahem—older age, I eat papayas like a human being. Here's the best way: Go to Hawaii. Forget your mainland grocery store, just go to Hawaii. Buy, or borrow, a firm yellow papaya and refrigerate it overnight. In the morning, take it out and slice it in half. Scrape the seeds out toward the stem end. Squeeze a healthy taste of lime (not lemon) onto it and eat it with a shiny silver spoon . . . slowly. Savor every tingle of taste. Eat both halves. You will think you are in heaven. And you will be. Trust me. Maika'i ke ola (life is good). Aloha!

BOOKS BY GRAHAM SALISBURY INCLUDE:

Blue Skin of the Sea: A Novel in Stories
Under the Blood-Red Sun

M*y mother loved to entertain. Quite often her guests would drink their tea or coffee without adding cream, so the half-and-half my mother always provided wouldn't be used. The next day she'd let me have the half-and-half to make what I thought was the best ice cream in the world. It has to be eaten soon after it's frozen or it will become very hard. Eating it quickly presented no problem for my younger sisters or for me.*

BOOKS BY JOAN LOWERY NIXON INCLUDE:

Candidate for Murder
Deadly Promise
Will You Give Me a Dream?

Extra-Creamy Lemon Ice Cream

2 teaspoons grated lemon rind
3 tablespoons lemon juice
1 cup sugar

1 pint half-and-half (milk can be
added to make a full pint)

Combine all ingredients and mix until sugar is dissolved. Pour into an ice cube tray (or metal pan similar in size) and freeze. It does not need to be stirred while freezing. Eat soon after mixture reaches freezing point. Serves 4.

My father tells me that he has been making this fudge since he was nine or ten years old. And so, at this writing, he has been whipping up a batch of fudge for some seventy years.

Watching him at work in the kitchen, waiting to taste the test, helping to stir, licking the wooden spoon, and eating my father's fudge are some of the most pleasant memories of my childhood and of my father. I'm so glad this project came along, because until now, the recipes for Norm's Fudge and Norm's Chocolate Fudge Coconut Balls have never been written down.

BOOKS BY JIM AYLESWORTH INCLUDE:

My Son John
McGraw's Emporium
Wake Up, Little Children
My Sister's Rusty Bike

Norm's Chocolate Fudge

2 cups sugar	$\frac{1}{2}$ cup white Karo syrup
$\frac{1}{2}$ cup milk	2 squares of unsweetened chocolate

Mix together ingredients in a cooking pot. Set at medium heat and bring to a boil (about ten minutes). Continue cooking, stirring occasionally, until the candy reaches a rolling boil.

To test if the cooking is done: Put an ice cube in 2 cups of water. Drop in a small amount of mixture and stir with fingers until the drops come together into a soft ball. Generally, 2 or 3 tests are necessary. Eat every test!!

When the test is okay, remove from heat and set pot to cool in cool water in the sink (about 10 minutes).

Add:

1 teaspoon vanilla	1 tablespoon butter
1 pinch salt	1 dash cinnamon

Stir-beat until the fudge loses its gloss and becomes stiff (15 to 25 minutes).

Pour into a buttered platter and cut into squares.

Norm's Chocolate Fudge Coconut Balls

Same as above fudge recipe, but let test be a little bit stiffer. Beat longer. Fudge should still be warm (hot), but workable.

Have marshmallows ready; cut in half. Have coconut ready.

Wash and butter your hands.

Put ½ marshmallow into fudge pan. Scoop out with a spoon an amount to cover marshmallow. Roll into balls, and roll the balls in the coconut. Work fast! It's easier with two persons.

Cheerio necklaces—my earliest fashion accessory and one of my mother's best recipes when I was growing up. The ingredients are basic—string and Cheerios. My mother would put the necklace on me in the morning—and by lunch it would be gone. Since she never lost the recipe, I was able to accessorize and munch each day.

BOOKS BY PAULA DANZIGER INCLUDE:
Amber Brown Is Not a Crayon
Amber Brown Goes Fourth
The Cat Ate My Gymsuit

When I was growing up, my friends enjoyed coming over to my house for one of my special meals. However, their enjoyment didn't come from the taste of the food. It came from the sight of it. (I was a horrible cook then and still am.) Take my advice. If you're not much of a klutz in the kitchen you can still make a meal interesting. Or, at least, a little scary. I've often wondered whether these meals from my elementary school days are among the reasons I've written so many books featuring monsters.

BOOKS BY STEPHEN MOOSER INCLUDE:
Elvis Is Back and He's in the Sixth Grade!
Young Maid Marion
The Creepy Creature Club Series
The Thing Upstairs

Eyeball Soup

1 can of tomato soup   10 grapes

Prepare soup following directions on can. Pour into a bowl. Plop in grapes. Serve with a diabolical chuckle.

Vampire Brain Delight

spaghetti   large ceramic bowl
red spaghetti sauce   poster paint

Paint the face of Dracula on the outside of the bowl using poster paint. Boil spaghetti till soft. Drain. Place in bowl. Pour in spaghetti sauce from jar. Stir. Dare your guests to scoop Dracula's brains onto their plate. They will, if they are hungry enough.

Robert Quackenbush

$\mathcal{D}$*etective Mole is the star of several mysteries I have written and illustrated about his adventures. His books include* Detective Mole and the Halloween Mystery, *which won an Edgar Allan Poe Special Award for best juvenile mystery. He came to be when my son, Piet, was a child and liked to pretend he was a detective. Piet gave me the ideas for mysteries for Detective Mole to solve, so there was often a lot of talk around the house about what the good detective would do about this situation or that—even when it came to figuring out what he would like to eat. Piet thought of these recipes (with his mother's help), since pizza and bananas was his favorite food back then. In those days Piet's lunch with Detective Mole was practically a daily event. Enjoy!*

BOOKS BY ROBERT QUACKENBUSH INCLUDE:

Detective Mole and Miss Mallard mysteries
Henry the Duck series
Lost in the Amazon: A Miss Mallard Mystery
Batbaby
Henry's Awful Mistake

Lunch with Detective Mole

MAIN COURSE: CLOAK-AND-DAGGER PIZZA

4 English muffins, cut in half	1 teaspoon basil
a few drops olive oil	1 tablespoon chopped dried onion
8 tablespoons spaghetti sauce	8 slices mozzarella cheese

1. Toast English muffin halves in a toaster.
2. Put olive oil in small pan over a low heat and add spaghetti sauce, basil, and dried onion. Cook until sauce is hot and bubbly.
3. Spread 1 tablespoon sauce on each muffin half.
4. Place cheese on top of the sauce, 1 slice on each muffin half.
5. Place muffins on a cookie sheet in a 350° F oven until the cheese melts, about 10 to 15 minutes.

Serves 4 (two pizza halves for each person).

DESSERT: CHILLING BANANA DELIGHT

4 bananas	½ cup grated coconut

1. Peel bananas and wrap each separately in foil.
2. Put in the freezer for at least 3 hours, until frozen hard.
3. Remove from freezer, unwrap banana, and roll in coconut.
4. Eat like a Popsicle. Serves 4.

BOOKS ILLUSTRATED BY RICHARD JESSE WATSON INCLUDE:
Tom Thumb (also wrote)
The Dream Stair

Cats' Eyeballs in Blood
(with gold nuggets)

The following recipe requires ingredients to be obtained
if at all possible from Spanish pirate ships:

1 can tomato soup   1 cup cubed sharp cheddar cheese
1 cup (more or less) KIX cereal

Optional, if adults are willing to walk the plank:

¼ cup fresh (preferably) or dry basil   1 clove fresh garlic
    pinch red pepper flakes

Cook the soup as Grama Campbell suggests (add squashed garlic if you're into garlic). Put it into bowl. Add pepper flakes if you are swarthy. Add basil if you are dashing. Dump in the cats' eyeballs (KIX). The longer they bob around, the slimier they get. Add as many gold nuggets (cheese) as you think you can afford.

COMPANION DRINK: BANANA MILK SHAKE:

4 scoops vanilla ice cream   1 teaspoon real Mexican vanilla
1 cup milk

COMPANION SALAD FOR ALL WORTHY SKIPPERS:

1 avocado   salt and fresh ground pepper
1 tablespoon lime juice

Cut avocado in half, remove seed, douse with lime juice, salt and pepper to taste, and eat it with a thin tablespoon. Cradle the avocado in the palm of your hand and scoop the mysterious food right down your gullet. For an added salivary scream, splash on Tabasco.

If you are concerned with the high fat content of avocados, ask yourself, "Would any self-respecting pirate worry about getting splinters from a treasure chest?"

I *consulted my two sons as to which scrumptious delicacies they remembered their loving, creative, gourmet-cooking, Jewish mother preparing especially for them. One answered, "Shake and Bake." The other said, "Hamburger Helper." I don't remember that! I remember hours in the kitchen! I remember making chopped liver.*

BOOKS BY RUTH HELLER INCLUDE:

Animals Born Alive and Well
The Reason for a Flower

Chopped Liver

1 pound chicken livers   2 hard-boiled eggs
1 large, raw onion   salt to taste

Boil chicken livers for 10 minutes. Drain. Grind in electric mixer with eggs and onions—not too smooth; retain a little texture. Add salt to taste. Spread on matzos. If spred on crackers, call it "pâté."

❧·❧· INDEX OF RECIPES ·❧·❧

❧· INDEX OF CONTRIBUTORS ·❧